A CONVERSATION
about
OHIO UNIVERSITY
and the
PRESIDENCY

❦❦

1975–1994

Claire and Charles Ping in front of a portrait of the first president of Ohio University, Rev. Jacob Lindley, hanging above the fireplace at 29 Park Place, their new home. They are dressed for a formal dinner marking the inauguration of Dr. Ping as the eighteenth president and Mrs. Ping as the first lady of Ohio University, March 6, 1976.

A CONVERSATION
about
OHIO UNIVERSITY
and the
PRESIDENCY

❧ ❧

1975–1994

Charles J. Ping

Interviews conducted by Samuel Crowl
With an additional interview by Doug McCabe

OHIO UNIVERSITY LIBRARIES
Athens

© 2013 by Ohio University Libraries

Ohio University Press, Athens, Ohio 45701

ohioswallow.com

To obtain permission to quote, reprint, or otherwise reproduce or distribute
material from Ohio University Press publications, please contact our rights and
permissions department at (740) 593-1154 or (740) 593-4536 (fax).

Printed in the United States of America

Ohio University Press books are printed on acid-free paper ™

23 22 21 20 19 18 17 16 15 14 13   5 4 3 2 1

Unless otherwise noted, all photographs are from the University Photographer Collection,
Mahn Center, Ohio University Libraries.

Cover photo of Charles Ping: Ben Siegel/Ohio University

Cover photo of Sam Crowl: Lauren Pond/Ohio University Libraries

Library of Congress Cataloging-in-Publication Data

Ping, Charles J.
A conversation about Ohio University and the presidency, 1975–1994 / Charles J. Ping.
    pages cm
Includes bibliographical references and index.
ISBN 978-0-9650743-8-4 (hc : alk. paper) — ISBN 978-0-9650743-9-1 (electronic)
1. Ohio University—Presidents—Interviews. 2. Ping, Charles J.—Interviews. 3. Ohio
University—History. I. Title.
LD4191.O817P567 2013
378.771'97—dc23

2013029587

This book was funded in part through

The Vernon R. and Marion Alden Library Endowment

The Beth K. Stocker Library Fund

and with additional financial support from

Ohio University Libraries

Executive Vice President and Provost's Office

and

University College

CONTENTS

ILLUSTRATIONS

ACKNOWLEDGMENTS

THE TEXT THAT follows is largely an edited version of the transcript of videotapes recorded in May and June 2011. It is a conversation between two old friends. Three voices are heard, principally mine and that of Sam Crowl, Shakespeare scholar, professor of English literature, former chair of the Faculty Senate and dean of University College, and now Trustee Professor emeritus. Then in a final session the person commenting and asking thought-provoking questions is Doug McCabe, curator of manuscripts in Ohio University Libraries' Mahn Center for Archives and Special Collections.

Sam is the interlocutor, and without Sam's insistence none of this would have been recorded. Only Sam could have elicited these responses or opened my inner thoughts. He shared many of the events and helped make change possible. Our friendship, which stretches back more than thirty-five years, is a relationship of shared respect, trust, and affection.

I am deeply indebted to a whole host of named and unnamed trustees, faculty, staff, and alumni who led the way forward and made these years good for me and my family and, I believe, for Ohio University. The contributions of three provosts, Neil Bucklew, Jim Bruning, and, close to the end of my years as president, Dave Stewart, were critical to all that was good in those years.

Scott Seaman, dean of University Libraries, was supportive right from the start of this project, and without his help and the dedicated work of Library staff, in particular Kate Mason, coordinator of communications and assistant to the dean, who managed the project and was the primary copyeditor, this manuscript would never have been completed. She was ably assisted by Rob Dakin, records management associate, and by graduate assistants Lena Chapin and Krithika Rajaraman. Bill Kimok, university archivist and records manager, searched the archives and identified photographs from the period. He was ably assisted by Janet Carleton, digital initiatives coordinator, and graduate assistants Kate Munsch and Lauren Pond in the digital image processing. I am grateful to them all for their assistance.

Three introductions, each written from a different perspective, contribute much to the conversations: Jim Bruning from the perspective of an active agent for change and progress; Betty Hollow, who knows the history of Ohio University from her search of its rich archives and has captured much of that history in her bicentennial celebration, *Ohio University, 1804–2004: The Spirit of a Singular Place;* and Sam Crowl, who kept the conversation moving. I am grateful to all three for taking time to write the introductions, and for what they add to the conversation.

Doug McCabe patiently followed and produced the whole series of conversations, presiding behind the camera for all but the last session, when he skillfully took over for Sam Crowl.

Finally, I want to acknowledge, with love and gratitude, Claire, who made all this possible. I do so by dedicating this book to her using the honorary degree citation, endorsed by a committee of faculty and students, adopted by the University trustees, signed by Charlotte Eufinger, then chair of the board of trustees, and read at my last commencement, June 11, 1994. It is the only time I remember kissing an honorary degree recipient.

OHIO UNIVERSITY

June 11, 1994

HONORARY CITATION

presented to

CLAIRE O. PING

*Your dedication as Ohio University's First Lady is seen and
felt in the life of the University and the community.*

*Your grace and style have endeared you to thousands of students, faculty, and guests
of the University, whether in your home, across campus, or around the world.*

*Our community and the quality of life we enjoy is greater today because of the time
and talents you have given to the community as well as to the campus, including
such projects as the Dairy Barn, Downtown Revitalization, Holiday Decorations,
Baker Center Improvements, the Kennedy Museum, and numerous others.*

*Above all else we honor you for caring and for your love of people. The extended
University family became your family; the Athens community became your home.*

*In recognition of your achievements and
by virtue of the authority of the Board of Trustees
Ohio University confers upon you the honorary degree,*

DOCTOR OF HUMANE LETTERS
with all the rights and privileges pertaining hereunto.

Charles J. Ping
President

Charlotte Coleman Eufinger
Chairman of the Board

A CONVERSATION
about
OHIO UNIVERSITY
and the
PRESIDENCY

❧ ❧

1975–1994

INTRODUCTION

❧ ❧

James Bruning

I ARRIVED AT Ohio University in the fall of 1962 as a new PhD faculty
member. That year turned out to be the beginning of one of the best
financial times here at OHIO. A youthful and energetic Vernon Alden
had been inaugurated as president, and during the years of his presidency,
enrollments rose dramatically, from 9,500 to nearly 20,000. Money flowed
from tuition, state subsidies, and a variety of research, training, and economic
development grants. Expansion and growth were taking place everywhere on
campus. Dormitories to house the enormous influx of students were built,
and since the flood of students was expected to provide an endless source of
income, these buildings were financed through the sale of bonds.

Ten years later, during the tenure of President Claude Sowle, a financial
crisis began that almost destroyed the University. In less than five years, for a
variety of reasons, enrollment dropped to less than 13,000. As a result of that
precipitous enrollment drop, the endless source of income abruptly ended,
since almost all of the monies to operate the University came from student
tuition and enrollment-based state subsidies. Because of the enrollment decline, those sources of university income were reduced by nearly one-third. At
the same time, the bonds that had been sold to pay for construction of the
dormitories came due, even though many of the buildings were nearly empty.

As a way of dealing with the financial crisis, President Sowle instituted a
review process that he termed "open budget hearings." Budget unit heads had
to present and to defend their budgets publicly so that any "fat"' would be open
for review and critique. All members of the university community could attend

these hearings and "suggest" where greater cuts should be made. Since any reductions in another budget might mean less taken from yours, outrageous comments and suggestions became the norm. Mean-spirited finger-pointing at the "fat" (which almost always meant eliminating more personnel) in other units was typical of the hearings. Terminations of large numbers of staff and untenured faculty resulted in an almost complete breakdown of collegiality and cooperation among the various administrative, service, support, and academic groups on campus. The campus climate was permeated by suspicion and hostility. Students on campus engaged in a variety of protests and demonstrations to save favorite programs. The aggressive or clever heads of administrative units tended to be treated less severely in the budget reduction process than those who were cooperative and open. One of the jokes on campus was, "If you want to defend your budget successfully, you have to be a gorilla or a guerrilla—you'll have to decide which tactic works best."

Divisiveness among the academic schools and departments resulted largely because of the budget cuts to those units that were made on the basis of student enrollments, or more specifically, weighted student credit hours. I was a department chair at the time, and we chairs and school directors quickly learned that the way to reduce the cuts to our budgets was to increase, or at least protect, our student enrollments. Attempts to draw (a nice word for steal) majors and enrollments from other departments became the norm, and cooperation among departments came to a halt.

With such a difficult social and budgetary environment, there is no doubt that President Charles J. Ping came to Ohio University during the worst of times. As Charlie phrases it in the first segment of the interviews with Professor Crowl, "The University teetered on the edge of default." That assessment was true of both the social climate on campus and the financial situation.

Charlie's first challenge was the immediate and desperate financial crisis. If one reviews the titles of his annual convocation addresses[1] and then listens to his reflections in *A Conversation about Ohio University and the Presidency, 1975–1994*, it is clear that Charlie had an amazing ability to deal with immediate problems and yet to deal with those problems within a broader context of the future of the University. One can see this in his earliest convocation addresses. Although delivered to a dispirited faculty and staff, those addresses were positive and solution oriented. The initial two were titled "Defining Issues and Shaping the Future" and "The Tasks Before Us." In his third address, he emphasized the "Search for Community," a recognition of the importance of working together to solve the difficult problems that the University faced. Collectively, his convocation addresses describe President Charles Ping: a president who dealt with many immediate crises. He was never caught up by them, and he always maintained his vision for Ohio University's future.

As the overall situation at Ohio University stabilized and gradually improved, Charlie's annual addresses began more clearly to reflect his fundamental belief that Ohio University could and should be an institution of extraordinary quality and excellence. His reflections clearly reveal that throughout his presidency his primary goal was to enhance the quality of the educational and intellectual experience at Ohio University. This concern for quality ranged from student life on campus, to undergraduate general education in the arts and humanities, to decisions involving the most research-focused PhD programs. He was consistent in his belief that the broad-based planning process, which he termed "holistic," should serve as the vehicle to guide decisions and should be driven by intellectual ideas. This planning process also had to have "cash value" and be part of the budget process. Planning and goal setting were central to Charlie's administrative style, and those plans and goals were expected to demonstrate observable results.

The vehicle for this planning process was the University Planning Advisory Council, or as it was generally known, UPAC. This group was made up of several administrators, faculty and students, the Faculty Senate Executive Committee, and three of the academic deans. UPAC was charged with developing a complete set of income and expenditure recommendations that would serve as the basis of the university budget for the following year. Each year, as part of this planning process, funds were set aside for new initiatives and investments. All departments, in all areas of the University, were encouraged to submit proposals. When a proposal was funded, the unit accepted the responsibility. Each proposal had to include measures that would later be used to determine the return on the planning pool investment.

Proposals were evaluated in the context of a series of holistic criteria that emphasized cooperation, quality, and promotion of the overall good of the

University. Special credit was awarded to proposals authored by multiple departments or by budget units. In this simple way, "cash value" for cooperation came to be the norm, and the planning pool served as a vehicle to break down the old animosities that lingered from the open budget hearings.

As reflected in the discussions with Professor Crowl, the themes of "Quality," "High Expectations," and "A Stubborn Striving for Excellence" clearly were the guiding principles for Charlie's presidency. These also were the titles of his later presidential addresses to the Ohio University community. There is no doubt that Charlie's greatest source of pride and accomplishment centered on the intellectual growth and educational experience that he felt made Ohio University unique. Special pride is obvious when he talks about the growth of the Libraries, the outstanding research programs at Ohio University, the general education program, the importance of cooperation and collaboration, the development of the Centers of Excellence, and especially the international programs that ranged from Africa, to Southeast Asia, to the Far East.

The second segment of the discussions with Professor Crowl is devoted largely to the faculty, alumni, and friends of Ohio University whose time and generosity helped make a large number of special goals become a reality. Charlie discusses a remarkable group of alumni and friends who contributed their time and, especially, their resources. These people made possible sources of quality such as the 1804 Fund, Cutler Scholars, and Eminent Scholars as well as a wide variety of programs ranging from a new approach to general education, to new or completely revitalized colleges in health sciences, engineering, and osteopathic medicine, to specialized research programs ranging from genetic engineering to physics. He also talks about the people who provided invaluable leadership to ensure success of the 1804 and the Third Century campaigns, the Innovation Center, the Alumni Center, the revitalized Alumni Association and alumni board, and the gift of the beautiful Japanese cherry trees planted along the Hocking River. In a more humorous vein, he also talks about the reciprocal gift of Ohio University squirrels to Japan.

In addition to the long list of special people who gave so much of their time and talent to help bring Ohio University back from the depths of those worst of times, there also is discussion of an equally remarkable group of state, national, and international dignitaries who visited Ohio University at the invitation of Claire and Charlie. By bringing these illustrious civil rights leaders; authors; educational and university visionaries; state, national, and international dignitaries; and former presidents to campus, Claire and Charlie further enhanced the visibility and reputation of Ohio University.

The final interview is conducted by Doug McCabe and focuses on Charlie's continuing love of being a true academic, his love of philosophy as an academic discipline, and the application of philosophical principles as guides for life. Included in these academic reflections are Charlie's observations on the importance of what many might consider the more mundane, the student extracurricular activities that make up an integral part of the intellectual and educational college experience. These activities range from intercollegiate and intramural athletics, to fraternities and sororities, to a whole host of student organizations. Charlie saw all of these as a necessary part of college life that made up the fabric of Ohio University. In Charlie's view, each contributed to and promoted the educational and intellectual experience at Ohio University.

Throughout *A Conversation about Ohio University and the Presidency, 1975–1994*, there clearly are consistent themes of Charlie's concern for quality, excellence, careful goal-oriented decision making, and holistic planning driven by intellectual ideas. The viewer/listener will be struck by the breadth of Charlie's interests, his sense of humor, and his remarkable ability to tolerate, respect, and get along with everyone at all levels of the University. His personal demeanor and honesty generated trust. Existing adversarial relationships were diminished, and largely eliminated, by his steady, honest, and open personal style of dealing with others. A good example of this is recounted by Charlie and involves a joking comment by one of the chairs of the Faculty Senate who told him, "You know, you're not really as bad as I thought you were." Put in the context of the toxic environment of just a few years before, it was a genuine compliment.

Charlie's ability to eliminate suspicion and replace it with trust extended well beyond the compliment cited above. I served Charlie as provost for eleven years, and shortly before I retired, I met with the Faculty Senate Executive Committee regarding the UPAC appointments and the upcoming UPAC meeting schedule. As we were leaving, the chair of that year's Faculty Senate said to me, "You know, we really do trust you and Charlie. Why don't we just skip the UPAC process this year? You and Charlie should go ahead and write the final UPAC report that will be taken to the board. After you have finished writing it, give it to UPAC for review and comment. By doing that, we can save hours of meeting time." While I didn't accept the offer, and assumed it was made in jest, all I could think of was, "How far we have come with Charles J. Ping as president."

Note

1. Charles J. Ping, *Ohio University in Perspective: The Annual Convocation Addresses of President Charles J. Ping,* 2 vols. (Athens: Ohio University Press, 1985, 1994).

INTRODUCTION

Betty Hollow

I N LATE 1974, members of Ohio University's presidential search committee faced the task of finding a new leader for their beloved but belea-
guered school. They had no illusions that the job would be easy, for this
"glamour" school of the 1960s was now widely known as a "troubled campus." In the preceding five years, enrollment had fallen—unexpectedly, dramatically, and repeatedly—from a high of 22,900 (total enrollment) in 1969–70
to 13,600 in 1974–75. The loss of revenue from student fees, combined with
uncertain and fluctuating allocations from the state, had resulted in a seemingly endless round of budget cuts, the loss of both faculty and staff positions, and an untenable financial situation. According to Alan Booth, chair of
the search committee and of the Faculty Senate, which had recently passed a
resolution on collective bargaining, "Morale was worse than anything I could
imagine." His committee hoped to find solutions in a competent new administrator. What they knew they needed was a miracle worker.

That they found Charles J. Ping—college athlete, ordained minister, ex-
perienced teacher and administrator—was a miracle in itself. He had been
suggested as a candidate for the Ohio University presidency but had asked to
have his name removed from consideration. Oddly enough, the search committee kept his name on their lists, but not as a top contender. Instead, concerned that most of his experiences had been at small, private schools and that,
as an intellectual and a philosopher, he might not be tough enough to handle
Ohio University's problems, they put his name on a list of "reservists."

However, by early 1975 Charles Ping had become the group's leading candidate. By all accounts, he had been successful in his six years as provost at Central Michigan University. He had used creative approaches in negotiations with the new faculty union (the first at a four-year state school); he had encouraged and guided the development of a new curriculum with general education at its core. He had taken time to attend Harvard University's Institute for Educational Management, both as a participant and as a mentor to other educators, and in the winter of 1975, he was back at Harvard enrolled in another graduate management program—in this case, one that focused on corporate rather than educational issues. Given his varied experience and enhanced credentials, his supporters at Central Michigan expected that within the year he would be their new president.

Instead, in September 1975 Charles J. Ping began his nineteen-year tenure as the president of Ohio University. The search committee, having tracked him down at Harvard, had been impressed with his commitment to long-range planning, his experience with collective bargaining, his obvious intelligence, and his confidence that problems could be solved. He had been impressed with their deep commitment to and affection for the school they represented and with their willingness to place their trust in him. A visit to Athens offered a glimpse of the school's beautiful setting, and a review of its long, often tumultuous history revealed its unique characteristics. Here, isolated in the hills of Southeast Ohio, was a school with strong international connections. Here, where the emphasis was on undergraduate education, were thriving professional schools, graduate programs, and research labs. Here, though disillusioned and dispirited, was a strong, young faculty that was in danger of losing its newest recruits because, as a former trustee lamented, "the whole place was bankrupt and didn't know it."

What had happened that could "bankrupt" a thriving school within five short years? For some, the answer is simple: "The '60s happened," and it is true that the great social upheavals of the decade—the explosion of college enrollments fed by baby boomers, the civil rights movement, the increasing opposition to the war in Vietnam—reverberated in events on Ohio University's campus not only in the '60s, but well into the '70s.

The baby boom, which was the reason for Ohio University's exciting, enormous expansion, also created serious long-term problems for Ohio University. In 1961, OHIO's Athens campus, with fourteen new dormitories, five new classroom buildings, a new student center, physical education and health centers, and natatorium, was adequate for its 9,600 students, but incoming president Vernon Alden knew that within the next ten years that number would double. The pressure was on to provide more new facilities, especially housing, for a horde of new Bobcats.

When President Alden was inaugurated in 1962, an East Green housing complex was more or less complete. Six new dorms were under construction on the West Green and nineteen more, financed with bonds, were planned for a complex on the South Green. Construction was loud, messy, and continuous, but demand repeatedly outstripped supply. Freshmen, who were required to live on campus, were crammed into triples that were built as doubles. The *Post* editor declared the dorms "jammed past capacity" and also condemned the policies that forced upper-class students to live in approved off-campus housing until age twenty-three and women to obey "paternalistic" hours. In 1964, hundreds of students poured onto the College Green to denounce the University's housing policies, which, they said, were designed to "encroach on our freedoms." Ten years later, many of Ohio University's dorms would stand half empty, creating a seemingly unsolvable financial problem for Charles Ping's administration.

A second national phenomenon affecting Ohio University in the '60s and '70s was the civil rights movement. President Alden's administration had actively recruited students of color, integrated the dorms, and publicized its nondiscriminatory admissions policy in the 1964 catalog. There were more African American students on campus than there had ever been, but they remained a community within a community, depending on each other for academic and emotional support and for most of their limited social life.

They did, however, follow the progress of the civil rights movement from the sit-ins of the early '60s, to the riots in Watts and Detroit, to Martin Luther King's philosophy of nonviolence, to Stokely Carmichael's insistence on Black Power. By 1968 some Ohio University students, including black student leader James Steele, were declaring their allegiance to the movement. Steele openly criticized the Alden administration for touting integration but making no real commitment to it and challenged the Athens mayor to eliminate "vicious" racial discrimination by local landlords. In early 1969, Steele and members of

Ohio University's Black Student Action Coordinating Committee demanded that the University provide financial aid, if needed, for every African American student it admitted and create a black dormitory, a black curriculum, a black scholarship program, a black resource center, and a black student growth fund drawn from student fees. By April, President Alden had pledged $250,000 for a Black Studies Institute. In spite of this commitment, Ohio University's black students continued to feel sidelined, and tensions between blacks and whites, especially in the dorms, remained an issue into the '70s. In 1974, a list of new demands by a group of black students was the proverbial last straw in a series of crises that led President Claude Sowle to resign.

As the civil rights movement became more violent, so did the war in Vietnam and demonstrations against it. By 1965, students across the country were burning draft cards. A year later some Ohio University professors were holding teach-ins to discuss US involvement in Asia, and an editorial in the *Post* said, "Let's withdraw." In October 1969, thousands of students filled the College Green to observe national Vietnam Moratorium Day, and a month later the country's largest antiwar rally drew some of them to Washington, D.C. There was no way to know that within six months Ohio University would experience a prolonged, violent protest that would leave it with the reputation of a "militant" campus.

But even before the end of the '60s, a careful observer could have anticipated that some internal campus issues that did not seem so significant in and of themselves would, in combination, eventually become toxic. For example, a costly strike by nonacademic workers in 1967 was not settled until after the University was forced to close, resulting in widespread negative publicity. Resolutions from the Faculty Senate protesting construction of the Convocation Center and the switch from semesters to quarters were never forwarded to the board of trustees, alienating many faculty members. Continuing demands, demonstrations, protests, and drug use by students, along with the *Post*'s outspoken editorials, had disgusted parents, taxpayers, and legislators. Funds that had seemed easily available seemed to be drying up.

In February 1969, Governor James Rhodes proposed a budget for Ohio University that provided no increase in revenue from the previous year, creating a $1.5 million shortfall. Two weeks later, the board of regents presented a new funding formula that eliminated the state subsidy for out-of-state students and institutional grants for poor families. Elimination of this subsidy was particularly insidious for Ohio University because approximately 25 percent of its students were from other states. In March, a report from the board of regents said that Ohio legislators were considering sixteen bills related to higher education, "most of which were of a punitive nature." In April, HB 251 proposed allowing the regents to establish enrollment levels, faculty workloads, and standards for both academic and administrative personnel. Not surprisingly, Ohio University's Faculty Senate was as bitterly opposed to this idea of centralization as they were to the reality that Ohio, then ranked fifth of the fifty states in income, was forty-fifth in its support of higher education. By the end of the year, the senate, along with Ohio University's new president, Claude Sowle, were equally dismayed when Governor Rhodes announced his plan, made without consultation with the state's universities or the board of regents, to turn six of Ohio's two-year schools into full-fledged four-year institutions, allowing them to compete with existing state universities.

President Sowle, who had served as dean of the University of Cincinnati's law school and written about the problems of student unrest, recognized that the mood in Columbus, rising inflation, a stagnant budget, and the growth of the student body to 22,900 presented challenges. He pledged himself to an open administration that included faculty and students in decision making and defined the University's role as developing students' maturity, ability to perceive and analyze issues, and "courage to act when they feel it is necessary." He organized six task forces to complete a sweeping self-study of the University's needs—the first in the school's history—and announced measures to plug the budget deficit: a limit on new hiring (including much-needed faculty), the sale of five of the University's six airplanes, and an increase in student fees. The results were unexpectedly explosive. Faculty members protested that the student-faculty ratio was nearing an unacceptable 30:1. The trustees refused to approve sale of the planes until Sowle threatened to resign. Students opposed the fee increase with a takeover of the first floor of Cutler Hall and a standoff with the Athens police.

In the spring, to try to engage disaffected students, the faculty approved a new lenient "ABC" grading system for freshmen, an innovative Bachelor of

General Studies degree, a Residential/Experimental College, and an Honors Tutorial College—in essence, creating something for everyone and setting up a debate on innovative versus traditional pedagogy. Nevertheless, approximately one-fourth of Ohio University's 1,000 black students drew up a list of grievances related to the Black Studies Institute, and nine antiwar protesters disrupted an ROTC class. In April, after President Richard Nixon ordered troops into Cambodia, demonstrations raged on campuses from Columbia to UC Berkeley, but at Kent State University the protests grew deadly on May 4, 1970, when Ohio National Guardsmen shot into a crowd and killed four students.

The fallout was immediate. Hundreds of universities and colleges closed within a few days, including all of Ohio's state schools except Ohio University. President Sowle, sure that Ohio University should stay open, appealed to students to avoid violence and sanctioned a "peaceful strike" and teach-ins. But over the next ten days, he and the university community lost their battle as, first, 2,500 students intimidated Court Street merchants on their March Against Death; then firebombs damaged ROTC offices in Peden Stadium, Chubb Hall was occupied, and small groups of students took to the streets to hurl bricks at Athens police amid swirling clouds of tear gas. Finally, on the night of May 14, after more threatened bombings, injuries, and desperation, Sowle was forced to call for the National Guard. Within twenty-four hours, students were gone; the crisis was over, but aftershocks continued.

With the reopening of classes in the fall, the administration focused on improving campus security, communication, and student participation in university governance. An ombudsman was appointed, and the *Campus Communicator* began reporting university events and decisions. But soon attention turned to reports from the six task forces appointed to assess the status of the University. The task force on Student Life drew fire immediately. Focused primarily on intercollegiate athletics, the report determined that its varsity teams cost the University $1.9 million of the $48 million budget—$1.1 million more than ICA figures suggested. The discrepancy lay primarily in the task force's inclusion of the standing debt of $500,000 on the controversial Convocation Center. The group recommended reducing all of Ohio University's varsity teams—except basketball—to club status. A majority of Bobcat supporters, including the trustees, were outraged and adamant, and finally Sowle reluctantly agreed to keep the athletic budget at its current level.

In January 1971, President Sowle presided over open, but controversial, budget hearings that were broadcast on radio to let Ohio taxpayers know how their tax dollars were being spent. During the two-day proceedings, deans and administrators presented the needs of their departments and tried to justify the costs. The resulting budget included a request for an additional $3,300,000 (8 percent) in state funds to offset the need to raise tuition. However, Governor John J. Gilligan had other ideas: he proposed raising tuition and having Ohio students repay their state subsidy after graduation. Ohio's legislators were no more helpful; by September, they still had not finalized appropriations for an academic year that had already begun. Without a dollar figure from the state for '71–'72, Sowle instituted a salary freeze and ordered departments to leave vacant positions unfilled. Other complicating events that fall were an unexpected nine-day strike by ASFCME Local 1699, a proposal from the Center for Afro-American Studies to fill all current and future vacancies with African Americans, and a demand from students to extend hours of visitation in dorms. The other news, which was not too alarming at the time, was that enrollment was down by 2 percent.

To make Ohio University more attractive, the administration abandoned *in loco parentis* regulations. Students could enjoy beer and open visitation in dorms, and women would have no "hours." The trade-off was that all freshmen and sophomores had to live on campus, regardless of age. In spite of these efforts, in the fall of 1972 enrollment fell from 18,774 to 17,549. Perhaps John Millett, former chancellor of the board of regents, was right: Ohioans were no longer willing to pay for a four-year education; the state should only provide a two-year "fair price" education; and those wanting more could take out loans at commercial rates.

Whatever the reasons—poor economy, drop in birthrates, competition from other Ohio schools, "an aura of permissiveness"—in the fall of 1971, there were 650 vacancies in the residence halls. The budget suffered immediate cuts of $1.1 million and a second cut of $1.9 million in winter quarter, reducing the budget for '72-'73 to $43 million and the University's condition "to a critical state." More positions and funds for student life were eliminated, and

Lindley Hall was converted into offices and classrooms. In the spring, the legislature granted a subsidy of $1 million to Ohio University to offset the loss of tuition, which helped. But freshman applications for fall '73 were down by 18 percent. The admissions office began an all-out recruitment effort.

That fall, Sowle presented Guidelines for the Future. Composed of thirty-eight long-range goals, it was Ohio University's first mission statement. Unfortunately, enrollment and the budget now took precedence over everything else; crisis management was the modus operandi. Only 7,000 of 9,800 dorm rooms were filled. Lindley Hall had already been converted into classrooms and offices, and now four residence halls were closed. Thirty-two vacant faculty positions went unfilled; pink slips went to sixty first- and second-year probationary faculty members, and soon thirteen tenured faculty members found their names on a list of professors to be let go. They and their colleagues, who had expected to be included in decision making, were stunned. As one senior professor said, "We felt we were in a crisis situation, and the faculty was being let go, the very heart and soul of the institution was being decided without any meaningful consultation." It would not be long before the Faculty Senate passed a resolution on collective bargaining and made plans to conduct a poll to gauge support for unionization.

Students, apparently, felt equally out of the loop but expressed their discontent in different ways. In May 1974, seven hundred students with campus jobs went out on strike, creating four days of disorder. Then, after a music festival, students lit fires in the middle of Court Street and attacked police who arrived to put them out. Ted Jones, who headed the city of Athens police force, called the rock-throwing crowd the "most vicious" he had yet encountered. A few days later, a coalition of twelve student groups called for the resignation of President Sowle and six of his top administrators. They justified their list of fifty-one demands by saying "the stands taken by the administration are counterproductive in creating an atmosphere where the entire University can grow and learn together." They demanded that Sowle respond within twenty-four hours.

On May 19, a group of two hundred Concerned Black Students held a rally on the College Green, marched through campus, and then went to Baker Center to find President Sowle. They called him out onto the porch and accused him of allowing racist texts in classrooms and of not providing sufficient funding for minority programming. At the end of the angry confrontation, the students left, shouting epithets at Sowle, who later said he had been given some "pretty healthy shoves." The following day, Sowle resigned, saying, "I should no longer ask myself or my family to serve the University under such insane conditions."

The university community was shocked. Dr. Edward Penson, vice president for academic affairs, empathized, saying the position of university president had become a magnet "for abuse, attack, and demands, demands, demands." The *Post*, Sowle's constant critic, commended him for opposing tuition-raising proposals by Governor Gilligan and Chancellor Millett of the board of regents. Sowle's legacy included the Honors Tutorial College, the Bachelor of General Studies degree, the development of the Office of Institutional Equity, and the position of university ombudsman.

After five years of conflict and crisis, Ohio University needed an interim president who could calm the waters. Economics professor Harry Crewson, with twenty-five years on the faculty, had the temperament, the "savvy," and the credentials to do just that. He was well known not just by the faculty, but by union leaders, city officials, and Ohio legislators. His approach to the presidency was low-key. He eliminated weekly press conferences and WOUB's call-in talk show, *Open Line*. Most notably, he also cancelled the open budget hearings, which had pitted departments against each other and eroded collegiality.

Though Crewson proceeded without undue publicity or fanfare, he was not afraid to take a stand. He balanced the *Post*'s opinions with news from the Office of Public Information. He turned a deaf ear to student protests against dorms for freshmen only; met some, but far from all, of the demands from United Student Workers; and nonplussed Citizens for United Farm Workers by serving both union and nonunion produce in cafeterias. He was not as easily able to address the faculty's deep concerns about job security: there had been 729 faculty members in 1973, and only 651 were expected to be on campus in the fall of '75. But he could support the board of trustees' decision to delay the faculty's election of a collective bargaining agent until a new president arrived.

The issue of funding could not be delayed. Ohio University was in desperate straits. Crewson, trustees, and others who had influence in Columbus lobbied legislators and regents for supplemental funds. It wasn't easy, for as the publisher of the *Athens Messenger* and strong supporter of Ohio University G. Kenner Bush said, the legislature "had just lost all confidence." They didn't have much confidence that the faculty or anyone at the University could come up with a solution. With enrollment estimates for fall '75 below 12,000, the regents told trustees to plan for a university of 10,000. Trustees called the idea "disastrous," for the school and for Southeast Ohio. Ohio University would lose programs, one-third of campus buildings, and membership in the MAC. They bargained, saying, "We are not afraid of change. We are not afraid of doing some things wrong. All we want is the opportunity to correct what is wrong." They pushed hard for special subsidies that would allow them to try to stabilize enrollment at 13,500 within four years. They promised to recruit aggressively, cut expenses, close more buildings, and raze others. They gained some time.

President Crewson's successful year ended with the announcement that Ohio University was to be the home of an osteopathic medical school whose benefits to the University, Athens citizens, and Southeast Ohio were expected to be enormous. Shortly after, Charles Ping arrived with his family: Claire, Andy, and Ann.

On September 19, Ping met with Ohio University's faculty and staff for the first time. According to a young reporter of the *Post*, "gravely curious eyes inspected the towering reserved Presbyterian minister about to take over an institution whose problems had almost run away with it."

The new president did not choose to address these problems—overwhelming debt, empty residence halls, the loss of trust between the school's varied constituencies, the possibility of a unionized faculty—at least not directly. Instead, in a relatively short speech, he spoke of Ohio University's strengths, which in recent years had been hard to recall. He spoke of the school's long, distinguished history, of the beauty of its residential campus set in the hills of Southeast Ohio, and of its unique programs. He was, in contrast to most members of his audience, optimistic.

He did, however, outline the means by which he hoped to lead the University back to what it could and should be—informed participation, careful decision making, tough choices, and a renewed sense of community. To the faculty's enormous relief, he left no doubt that in his universe education was the single mission of a university and that it would be just that at Ohio University.

The path back to stability, and finally to excellence, was hard and long. But Charlie Ping liked challenges, and he was patient. He gave his faculty time to decide against unionization. He worked with trustees and the legislature to devise a unique plan in which empty West Green dorms were essentially "sold" back to the state to be used as the home of the new osteopathic medical school. He used his gravitas, along with eloquent language, to reassure Ohio taxpayers that Ohio University was a safe and exciting place to send their children. He led two very successful fund-raising campaigns that provided new programs, innovative research, and scholarships. No wonder he became known as "the man who rebuilt a university."

Ping's turnaround of Ohio University was not actually a miracle; it just seemed like one. The details of his administration have been covered in news articles, in academic journals, and, most recently, in Florence Clark Riffe's excellent book, *A Philosophy of Community: Ohio University in the Ping Years, 1975–1994.* In these video interviews, Ping speaks informally with his colleague and friend, Professor Samuel Crowl, and gives the ultimate insider's view. He is serious. He is funny. He is an excellent storyteller. And in providing this record he once again tells the story that he told so often during his presidency, the story of a singular place with its own history, setting, and distinctive characteristics, a place he came to lead and to love.

INTRODUCTION

❦❧

Sam Crowl

B
ETTY HOLLOW HAS set vividly the social and historical context for Ohio University when Charles Ping became president, and Jim Bruning has outlined concisely the major themes of Ping's presidency and the processes he created for their accomplishment. This allows me the opportunity to present a more personal take on the man and the times and to revisit and revise similar remarks I contributed to Florence Clark Riffe's history of the Ping years: *A Philosophy of Community: Ohio University in the Ping Years, 1975–1994.*

I have known Charlie Ping for almost forty years. We have been friendly adversaries, fellow administrators (well, I worked for him as a dean), colleagues, mutual lovers of the London theater, sports fans, and friends. The most important bond we share is our joy in the life of the mind and our passion for Ohio University. It was a rare pleasure, then, to have the opportunity to participate in Ohio University Libraries' "A Conversation about Ohio University and the Presidency, 1975–1994" project devoted to the nineteen years of his presidency. The bulk of the interviews took place in May and early June of 2011 in the rather cool and cavernous Studio A at WOUB-TV, but they quickly warmed up as my questions prompted his generous and detailed responses. Soon it seemed just like two old friends reminiscing about their shared memories of Ohio University in the 1970s, '80s, and early '90s. More than once I was tempted to say to Charlie, as Falstaff does to Justice Shallow in Shakespeare's play *King Henry IV, Part Two*: "We have heard the chimes at midnight." Later, Doug McCabe, Alden Library's curator of manuscripts, conducted an additional interview to fill in the gaps and to add important queries of Ping's postpresidential activities. Ping's memories will be of particular interest to all the members of the university family and to future historians of the University and American higher education. They join previously published volumes of the recollections of Presidents John C. Baker and Vernon R. Alden.

The first words I heard Charlie Ping utter were "Sweet are the uses of adversity." It was May 1975, and I was driving home from campus listening to WOUB's broadcast of the news conference he gave after having been named the eighteenth president of Ohio University. He must have been responding to a reporter's question about why he was interested in taking the reins of such a troubled institution. I smiled at our good fortune in finding a president who quoted Shakespeare, but I wondered if any mortal was capable of leading the University out of the morass of debt and desperation it had been plunged into in the previous four years.

Susan and I joined the faculty in the fall of 1970. The University was bursting at the seams with students. The enrollment neared 18,000, having more than doubled in less than a decade. Many of the remarkable number of academic and residential buildings planned in the Alden years (a figure in the forties) were still being completed. And the Hocking River was being moved. We had come from Indiana University, a similarly historic and picturesque institution, but we quickly discovered that the undergraduates at Ohio University were more lively and sophisticated than their Hoosier counterparts. Over 25 percent of them came from out of state, with large contingents from New York, New Jersey, Pennsylvania, and Massachusetts, and the mix of students was stimulating and invigorating. But the community had also been traumatized by the events of the previous spring, when the University had been forced to close in response to the prolonged student disturbances that followed the shootings at Kent State. Our own department was big and bustling, with established scholars in several fields and a group of creative writers with national reputations. Other disciplines seemed equally vibrant. This was a University on the move. The future seemed limitless.

Then, as Betty Hollow indicates, the bottom fell out. In three quick, disastrous years the enrollment plunged from 19,000 to 13,000. The resulting financial crisis led to massive budget cuts, the dismissal of several hundred staff and many tenure-track faculty, and the creation of a raucous, rancorous atmosphere that pitted the faculty against the administration, redirected the student antiwar protest movement to internal university issues, and culminated in the resignation of President Claude Sowle in the spring of 1974. Harry Crewson, a longtime professor of economics and the former chair of the city council, was appointed acting president, and he and the vice president for academic affairs, Taylor Culbert, managed to hold the University together for a year while Faculty Senate chair Alan Booth and board member Jody Galbreath Phillips led a committee of trustees, faculty, students, and President Emeritus Vernon Alden in the search for a new president.

The board of regents was not sympathetic to our plight. Plans circulated to strip the University of its graduate programs and to limit enrollment to 10,000. Only the effective lobbying of Governor James Rhodes and key members of the legislative leadership by several influential alums managed to provide the additional funding necessary to help the University weather the storm as the search for the new president proceeded. On campus a serious effort, led from within, to unionize the faculty gained momentum. Such was the state of the University in the spring of 1975. Only Charlie Ping could have found such adversity "sweet." In fact, when he returned to Central Michigan (where he was serving as provost) after his first campus visit, he reported to Neil Bucklew that "the University is a little gem that just has some mud on it. When it is cleaned up, it will sparkle." It turned out that the University had a little more mud on it than he had at first realized.

But Ping relished a challenge, and what he and the University accomplished in the next two decades is one of the great stories of American higher education in the last third of the twentieth century. Much of the potential Susan and I sensed about Ohio University back in 1970—seemingly dashed by the events of middecade—was not only realized but dramatically exceeded. The University is now widely regarded, on the strength of academic quality and value, research productivity, library holdings, and endowment, as one of the top public universities in the country. Such, certainly in the state of Ohio, was not the perception in 1975. What happened in the Ping years to restore the University's confidence and put it back on the track to excellence?

Well there was some "sweetness" in the adversity. The University had a long and noble—if neglected—history; a handsome—if poorly groomed—campus;

a loyal—if discouraged—alumni; an adventuresome and heterogeneous—if nonselective—student body; and a productive—if dispirited—faculty. Three years of fiscal crisis and savage struggle for scarce resources, paradoxically, also created the potential for cooperation. All this Ping saw or sensed, and it turned out, in retrospect, to be an ideal environment to put into practice his philosophical commitment to developing a comprehensive planning process based on the idea of a university as a community that exceeded the sum of its parts. A more secure or prosperous institution might have given lip service to genuine reform while continuing on with business as usual.

But Charlie Ping turned out to be the right man, in the right place, at the right time. John C. Baker and Vernon Alden had created the academic structure and the physical plant for the modern Ohio University; it was left to Ping to shape its vision of the future. Ping did not save the University; he got the University to save itself—a far harder task. He did so in an unusual fashion. He did not try to impose a grand and rhetorically eloquent vision on the university community; rather he tried to establish a process. He called it, as Jim Bruning points out, "holistic planning," through which the various parts of the university community would contribute to defining goals and setting priorities and then gather the strength to act upon them. Many of us were skeptical. "Planning" and "process" are not terms that ring big bells for many academics, especially those of us educated in the traditional disciplines of the arts and sciences. Leadership was a word that had been discredited by national events in the '60s and '70s. But Ping led in his own unique fashion. He concocted a synthesis of the idealism he admired in Plato and Hegel with the management strategies he had picked up at the Harvard Business School. He used it to create a comprehensive planning process and then stepped aside to allow it to function even though it removed him from the focus of attention.

A personal example will illustrate. Faculty know that in most administrations, whatever the stated budget or planning process, if you really want support for a pet project you go directly to the president to make your case. My department chairman, the head of the University Library Committee and a man passionately committed to books, had long secured special funding for the Library by doing so. He tried the same thing with Ping. One afternoon he loomed in my office doorway and more in sorrow than in anger muttered through his substantial beard: "The man hates books." Ping, and not for the first or last time, had just said "No." Saying "no" is tough. All presidents and patriarchs want to be the source from which all bounty flows, but Ping was willing to take the abuse in order to make the planning process work by not making private deals that undermined the system. Ping cherished books and was as much a product of the ideas flowing from Renaissance humanism as my colleague, but he resisted the challenge of subverting the system he had put in place for the temporary gratification of saying "Yes." I wish my colleague had lived to see Alden Library, some fifteen years later, its budget boosted by funding provided by the University Planning and Advisory Committee created by Ping, invited to join the distinguished Association of Research Libraries in North America. In Ping's system, the university community, not the president, had made the Library a top priority.

It took time, and time and patience and prudent doing were the hallmarks of his administration, and gradually the university community came to know, and even better, to trust Charlie Ping. But it did not happen overnight. I vividly remember a rocky and contentious Faculty Senate meeting during my term as chair. Ping and his first provost, Neil Bucklew, had made a controversial administrative appointment that troubled many senators. At one point in the heated debate a longtime professor of physics rose and stammered: "You presidents are all alike. You make bad decisions like this one. Then you leave the University, and we're left with the problem of cleaning up the mess." I saw Ping set his jaw and thought to myself: This stubborn Irishman isn't going anywhere. Later, when several attractive opportunities to move on to other presidencies did arise, I silently thanked that physics prof every time Charlie and Claire decided to stay because I knew his challenge still rumbled in Ping's memory. And when that appointment did, in fact, turn out to be messy, Ping cleaned it up himself.

Ping enjoyed a vigorous intellectual debate and never backed down from a fight—particularly with the regents or legislature—but he preferred cooperation to confrontation. Long before "thinking globally" became a necessity (and a cliché), he encouraged education for interdependence and funded guidelines for UPAC, 1804, and the statewide Academic Excellence grants that encouraged interdisciplinary, even cross-college, proposals; His own administrative style stressed that the president and provost shared the office of the presidency and, aided by several accomplished provosts (Neil Bucklew, Jim Bruning, and

David Stewart), he made the idea, stolen from the corporate world, work. He believed in a sleek administrative structure (a provost, two vice presidents, a treasurer, a dean of students, and a director of development). They became known as the 11:30 Group as they met together at that time every day that Ping was on campus so that each would come to see the University through the multiple perspectives of their individual problems and responsibilities.

On the personal side, Ping shared the presidency with his wife. As Charlie went to work to restore the University, Claire became an equally compelling and indefatigable force in leading local citizen groups interested in restoring downtown Athens, ravaged by a series of fires in the early '70s and by the flight of many Court Street merchants as new malls were built east of town. She led a decade-long effort to get the owners (often absentee landlords) of the handsome nineteenth-century buildings that lined Court Street to restore them to something like their former glory. Claire presided over countless receptions and dinners that came with the presidential territory and carted the spouses of board of trustee and foundation board members to every scenic spot in Southeastern Ohio when they were on campus for meetings. Claire also helped recharge Charlie's batteries by whisking him out of town for a weekend every other month or so just to get him momentarily away from the fishbowl world they inhabited.

The University's renaissance was a remarkable experience not just to witness but to live. The decade of the 1980s saw undergraduate applications increase from 6,500 to 12,000; the median high school class rank of the entering class increased from the 60th to the 80th percentile; the freshman to sophomore retention rate increased from 67 percent to 85 percent; the enrollment gradually climbed back to almost 18,000; the endowment increased from under $2 million to almost $100 million; external research funds more than quadrupled, leading the University to be classified as a Research II institution by the Carnegie Foundation; faculty books and research discoveries were regularly reviewed or discussed in the *New York Times, Washington Post, Wall Street Journal,* and other national publications; and the University was repeatedly listed in the more prestigious college guides.

It is appropriate that Ping's legacy is honored in the two campus institutions that carry his name: The Charles J. Ping Student Recreation Center and the Ping Institute for the Teaching of the Humanities. Ping cherished, even if his old football knees sometimes refused to cooperate, Juvenal's classical ideal of "mens sana in corpore sano." The Ping Center is devoted to exercise and the health of the body, while the Ping Institute seeks to stimulate the mind's powers of reason and imagination in the art and craft of teaching. Ultimately, however, his spirit will be most lastingly served by the Cutlers Scholars Program, which he has led for the past eighteen years. When fully endowed by private gifts, the program, modeled on the Morehead-Cain Scholars program at the University of North Carolina and the Rhodes Scholarship program at Oxford, will fully fund fifty students a year in one of the nation's most attractive educational opportunities for our best and brightest.

I hope you will enjoy this return to the Ping years as much as I did in living them and then revisiting them in the interviews that follow.

CONVERSATIONS

Dr. Ping teaching a class, 1985.

CONVERSATION
with
SAM CROWL

ᝍ ᝍ

May 17, 2011

SC: Charlie, in 1975, Ohio University was in trouble. The University had lost almost one-third of its student population. There had been subsequent cuts across the University budget, faculty had been fired, staff had been let go, and times were still turbulent on this campus. The '60s hadn't yet stopped. What made you interested in coming to Ohio University in 1975?

CP: Sam, let me talk about that in a minute. First, let me make some comments about our assignment and then oral histories in general. Now, I'm in my eighties, and like most people my age, I talk a lot about the past. The past has more reality for me than the future. As I talk, I am sometimes on subject, and I am sometimes off subject, so please drag me back when I wander. The second thing, this is not going to be a polished statement— it's going to be off the top of my heart, and I hope my head. We tend to view the past through the prism of the present; the light is refracted by what we believe to be true. So often the things that we think may have been planned carefully were really the product of other factors far more important than planning.

So, I think, with those caveats and cautionary notes, you asked an interesting question, one I've been thinking about. My first contact with

27

Ohio University was a sort of pro forma, "You have been nominated. Are you interested?" And I wrote back, "Thank you very much, I am honored, but no." The trustees of the university that I was then serving agreed to send me to the Advanced Management Program (AMP) at Harvard, which is a three-month-long intensive program with participants cloistered for the whole experience; it is largely people involved in their last move in corporations. I was sort of the oddball in that crowd. I thoroughly enjoyed it, and found to my amazement how hard corporate people do work in terms of studying and preparing for class.

But anyways, I got a phone call from Alan Booth, a history professor at Ohio, then chairman of the search committee and chairman of the Faculty Senate. He said, "Charlie, if a portion of the committee flew to Boston, would you be willing to meet with them?" I said, "Well, that's very flattering. Of course, I would." So, they flew up, and we met in Vern [Vernon R.] Alden's office. Vern was the CEO of the First Boston Company, I think, at the time. It was a group that included people like Ed [Edwin L.] Kennedy and Jody [Joan Galbreath] Phillips, as well as Alan [Booth] and a couple of other trustees, all of whom cared very deeply about the place. Their commitment to Ohio University was the first thing that piqued my interest. We talked for two hours about whatever they wanted to discuss, and the meeting broke up. I thought it was warm and cordial.

Then there was a quick follow-up asking me if I would be willing to meet with the whole committee. I said, "Based on my experience with this group, yes. I'm intrigued by how important the University really is to you. However, I'll meet with the full committee on one condition. I am not yet a candidate, and nothing is to go back to Mount Pleasant, or elsewhere, about my being a candidate." They were anxious for me to see the campus and to meet with faculty.

Before the meeting broke up in Boston, Vern Alden said, "Come here for a minute, and let me show you something." There on the wall of his dressing area was a large plaque. Mounted on the plaque were rocks, bricks, and pieces of pipe. We stood in front of the plaque for a moment in silence, and I wondered to myself, "What in the world was this?" [laughs]

Vern said to me, "These are all the things that were thrown through my windows during my years as president at Ohio University. Marion [Alden] and I," he went on, "regard those years as the best years of our lives." I didn't understand at the time, but I do now. [laughs]

Anyway, I made the trip to Athens. We were surrounded by a great cloud of secrecy. I understood only later that Alan Booth pulled in a lot of chits from the *Post* and elsewhere to maintain the secrecy of the trip. We met with the full committee in Nelsonville and saw the campus. The committee had planned it well. We came into town to the home of a faculty member; he and his wife had children roughly the same ages as ours. One of the things that we wanted to talk about was the public schools. They arranged for Claire to have a quiet visit to the high school.

I had a tour of the campus. The first thing that caught my interest was the dedication of the people to the place, and the second, the quality of the people. I was really impressed with the faculty I met. Third, I very quickly, as most people do, fell in love with the place. As I began to grasp more of the history, I became intrigued—here in the Midwest, a campus that has a sense of history!

So I went back to Harvard, after this visit, with my interest level raised significantly. I went immediately to talk to some of the Ohio businessmen in the Advanced Management Program. Without exception, they said, "Oh I wouldn't touch that place with a pole—and I certainly wouldn't send my daughter there." There were four or five members of the AMP class from Ohio. Then I went to some of my friends on the Harvard faculty. From them I got the exact opposite reaction. "What a great opportunity—look into it and cherish it." So, this created an intriguing clash of perspectives.

I'm not sure whether this is my reading back into the past, or whether, in fact, I really sensed this: The things that were important to me, then and now, are a genuine commitment to teaching and the undergraduate experience; the search for some sort of core common experience. And secondly, I was already making a great many speeches about the issue of internationalizing the campus. All this was part of the fabric of the Ohio campus.

I discovered that quickly. Most of the things that were important to me, I found were important to the faculty here. For example, I don't think you can impose upon an institution an interest in the internationalization of a campus. It is either there as part of the campus life or it's not. If it's not there, you have to nurture such a commitment over many years. The Southeast Asia study program, the large population of international students, and the faculty who had lived [abroad], done research, and were genuinely committed to global perspectives, were much in evidence. Alan Booth impressed me; he authored the definitive history of Swaziland. I came to appreciate the depth of the campus commitment more over the years.

SC: I understand that those were the attractions, and those are the attractions that have drawn many of us then and subsequently to the University. So you became interested, and that interest led to you being named the new president. When did you discover that there were problems that maybe you didn't fully grasp when you had taken the position?

CP: Well, I know how to read a balance sheet, [laughs] and I studied the University's financial reports. The problems were self-evident. But, I also looked at the larger picture, and the picture was that Ohio was a low-tax state, a low-support state, and there was room for movement.

SC: You hoped.

CP: I hoped, yes. The legislature had in fact appropriated a sizable sum, some three to five million, as I remember the figure, and essentially said, "We're going to bail you out on these bonds." The University was tottering on the edge of defaulting on the residence hall bonds—and I hope we can talk more about that later. As I began to study the situation and to think about it, some of the reasons were so clear—the precipitous drop in enrollment followed the instituting of an out-of-state surcharge. Our out-of-state student population had dropped in half overnight. That needed correcting. I felt the problems, given the era that we were moving into, were addressable.

I frankly didn't fully understand the depth or seriousness of some of those problems. There's a wonderful line in John Baker's oral history where he says, "You know I arrived in Athens, and I got a number of surprises." Among his surprises: the College of Engineering had never been accredited; the College of Business had never been accredited; there were no PhD programs; and there was no structure in place for private giving. Yes, I think I fell in love with the place and the people and that's continued to the present, but I got some surprises!

SC: Beyond the indebtedness problem—the bonds with the dormitories —what were the immediate challenges that you faced both intellectually and academically, as well as financially?

CP: Well, there were a great many challenges and some surprises—more than some, a great many surprises. I used to go down to the Convo [Convocation Center] every once in a while and just kick it because I discovered as one of the early surprises, it was still on a construction loan which turned over annually, subject to whatever that year's interest rate was. I was intrigued by the potential of a medical school. The bill had worked its way through the legislature during Harry Crewson's brief but eventful presidency. The legislation actually took effect on November 17 after I was on campus. The bill called for a College of Osteopathic Medicine to be established here. I thought that this might well be a very strong base to bring about a brighter future because funding that went to medical education would also go to the basic sciences. The college would provide opportunities for research and outreach that held great promise for the future of the University.

But then we discovered, after carefully reading the legislation, that someone had managed to slip into the bill a provision that unless sixteen students were admitted within twelve months of the effect of this bill, there would be no further release of appropriations for the medical school.

That timetable is unheard of, you know. Seven years is a sort of standard minimum to plan for and to get a medical school started. We had to get a medical school off the ground in twelve months.

A core of people—the basic science faculty, and new clinical faculty in particular—coalesced around this effort. I quickly turned to a man from Michigan, with whom I had been friends for many years. He had been the chief of staff to the Senate Appropriations Committee in Michigan, and he also had been active with the group of osteopaths interested in establishing a college here. Gerald Faverman was a person who could get things done and done in a hurry, even if it meant running right over some people, which he did from time to time. But he got the job done. And sure enough we had faculty in place, a curriculum in place, and an admissions process in place. Thanks to a group led by such people as Dr. Frank Myers. The following fall, we admitted the first twenty-four students. Well, along the way, we had to persuade the Faculty Senate that they wanted a medical school. Some senators were afraid that it would be a drain on resources, when it was just the opposite. That was an immediate problem and their opposition an immediate surprise.

SC: Some of that, of course, as you had envisioned it, did come to pass. Not only the College of Osteopathic Medicine as something that has been powerful for our region, which had not been well represented in the terms of medical services, but also for the research possibilities.

CP: Yes.

SC: Was Tom Wagner already here on the faculty?

CP: He was already on the faculty, and illustrates both the challenge and the opportunity of combining basic science and medical education.

SC: Yes.

CP: But the equipping of the labs that were necessary for the work that he did, and many other factors, were interactive. One of the things we built into the planning was that the arts and sciences' basic science faculty that was here would be the basic science faculty for the early years of training the medical students. I think the College of Osteopathic Medicine has been a tremendous boon for the region. You know, they have large vans that offer services throughout the region; they have introduced vaccination programs for children and clinical services. I think the College brought people here, who wouldn't have come if it had not been for the medical school, good people for the faculty and staff.

SC: You also were confronted with a faculty that had not had raises, or much of a raise, in the past three or four years. I had seen their numbers decline, as I mentioned earlier, and there was a very strong effort under way to form a union. What was that like?

CP: Well, I had lived with a union at Central Michigan. I had tried very hard for six years at Central to make collective bargaining work as a decision-making process, which allowed university deliberative process to run in tandem and not intrude on each other. I naively thought that that was possible. I went all over the country giving speeches and writing papers with this idea in mind. At the end of six years of serious effort to make that happen, I decided that it was impossible.

So, I came with the intent to try to do everything I could to help the faculty understand what collective bargaining would mean for them, and, therefore, to encourage them to oppose it. I was told that 80 percent or more of the faculty in the previous year with a straw vote had voted overwhelmingly in favor. The first hurdle was that there was no state law and the trustees had to agree to hold an election. I argued, in subsequent years, before the legislature that if the state was going to have collective bargaining it's better to have a state framework. At that time, the decision to hold an election rested solely with the board. I argued with the trustees, "Give us a little time to study the issues, and then a vote. If we don't have

Decades-long friends President Charles Ping and Dean of University College Samuel Crowl, with the Program of Excellence Award for the General Education Program, 1990.

a vote, I think the festering anger in the faculty will be there for years to come."

Part of the anger was rooted in the collapse of the budget that led to a list of faculty, some of whom were tenured, some nontenured and some like you, Sam, who turned out to be among the real "stars" of the faculty. They were facing the prospect of termination. In one of my periodic visits before assuming office, but after I had accepted the presidency, I made the decision that this proposal had to be shelved; we put it aside. If that had happened, the scars would have been deep and would have taken generations, really, to heal.

SC: You were right, and fortunately it didn't happen. We could move beyond that. But back to the unionization vote, as I recall, there was a six- or seven-month period of debate and discussion that culminated in a vote finally in the spring of 1976.

CP: We did things in the way a faculty ought to do them. We had a reserve shelf list in the Library, and circulated lots of papers. At least the thoughtful people read some of the material and reflected on what unionization would mean. And, I think some minds were changed in the process.

SC: Obviously, because the vote was in the negative. I can't remember what the totals were, but my guess is that it was something like 370 to 320, so there was a 50-vote margin, when it had been, as you say, about an 80 percent—

CP: favorable.

SC: favorable in the straw poll in the year before. What else do you remember from that first year like the medical college and unionization and financial stability that you had to tackle head on?

CP: I knew from the start that we had to address the dormitory problem. The system was built with the presumption that it would have a 90 percent or better occupancy rate to pay the mortgage, that is, the bonds. But, the then current occupancy rate was about 60 percent. So there was a huge shortfall in income. I learned, and this was one of my daunting surprises, when you studied the bond instruments, those bonds had first claim on any income coming to the University other than appropriations, which means that tuition would have gone to pay the bond holders.

       Even more serious, the problem that I saw as I got to know the campus was the quality of student life in the residence hall. That it was "troubled" would be the kindest word. We definitely needed to change the student culture in the residence halls. It wasn't surprising that people didn't want to live in the dorms. To accomplish that, I brought in a new dean of students, who was one of your colleagues in the English department, Carol Harter. Her appointment caused great consternation on the part of the trustees and a few others. "You've got a management problem, and you're bringing in an English professor to handle it; one who has had no administrative experience." I went, "Uh huh." Because

Faculty member, dean, and vice president Carol Harter, 1982.

I thought the root of the problem was in fact the quality of residential life.

Over the next several years, the legislature in essence said, "All right, we've given you a special appropriation—solve your problem." That was a pretty large order. And, the release of the funds was subject to review by the board of regents. Periodically, I had to go and shuffle my feet and say, "Yes, Sir," to the regents, or "Yes, Ma'am," and they would release another chunk of the money.

I thought Carol was the best person to address the root problem— the quality of student life. She proved to be a very good manager as well. She took hold of the thing, and she began to look for cost savings. She looked at everything beginning with the presumption that every room would have a phone. Any student who wanted a phone, she insisted, could contract with the telephone company to get one. She discontinued linen services, and developed a whole bundle of serious reductions in cost. That was the beginning of a change in the quality of the life for those who lived in the residence halls. But the key was a stronger residence life program.

A second part of the strategy that we hit upon as we were developing a medical school and expanding other programs: We could very well take residence halls that were currently standing empty and convert them to other uses. So, the first unit in the medical school was, in fact, one of the empty West Green dormitories. It was ideal for incoming medical school students because it had its own food service and a large kitchen area.

There was a ring of walk-in refrigerators to store corpses in; you had an all-tiled floor sloping to the drains for a general anatomy lab. Plus you had a lot of small rooms that could be made into faculty offices. And, you could do the renovations quickly. We were under the gun to get it done. They were still pounding on walls and nailing things down when we opened the medical school in Grosvenor Hall, but it was usable space.

As part of the package, we had the legislature, over the next several biennia, buy units out of the residence hall debt pool, that is, to pay off with lump sums the bonded indebtedness. We lowered the annual bill for indebtedness of the system, I believe, by more than a half million dollars.

We included all the units that were presumed to be a part of the bonded indebtedness to pay off the mortgage, including Howard Hall. Howard Hall, we decided early on, had to be torn down. Howard Hall could not be converted to other uses because it had wooden joists and beams; plus it wasn't exactly an esthetically pleasing building. In any case, we tore it down. Some of the legislators never forgot the fact that non-existing buildings were in the bond package they bought. When I'd be testifying, from time to time some legislator would say, "Aren't you the president who sold us a building you had already torn down?" Then I'd go into my spiel about a bonded indebtedness. "Ah, that doesn't make sense to me. We bought a building that was no longer there," would be the legislator's reply. "Yes," I said, "but the debt was still there."

I think a concentrated emphasis to change the character of student life, a serious effort at cost containment, and finally the reduction in annual bonded indebtedness payments helped us in a matter of three or four years to solve the problem.

SC: When you came you brought with you, and I'm thinking now in this context of building an administrative team, you came with an idea that was, I think, new to this campus in creating a role of the provost, who subsumed under that title the sorts of duties that would have gone with the title of an executive vice president for academic affairs. But you made it clear that the provost and the president would share the Office of the President.

CP: Exactly.

SC: This was more like a business model with a CEO and a COO, and that was a new phenomenon here. I chaired the search committee that brought us that provost. The candidates thought it was an ideal way of organizing the offices of the president and the provost, but it all depended on the president being serious about that sharing and letting the provost have a series of responsibilities that could be independently addressed. Talk a bit about Neil Bucklew and your previous relationship with him at Central Michigan.

CP: Well, remember, I was cloistered with a whole large group of businessmen, and we were working our way through a series of cases. This was an idea that had been fermenting in my mind. It had actually been part of a model, without being defined, at Central Michigan when I was the provost there. I got to know Neil when he became a candidate for an appointment at Central Michigan. Central had this distinction of being the first single campus to negotiate a labor contract with the faculty. Neil had just completed his PhD at Wisconsin in mediation and labor relations, and he had all the knowledge that I lacked about the intricacies of labor relations, so I brought him on my provost staff at Central to implement that first contract. He proved to be a superb administrator, and he negotiated a couple of additional contracts for us.

It's tempting to tell one story: Neil was negotiating a contract that involved a union demand that they get universal fees from the faculty that they were serving in order to be able to better serve them—a union shop. I was adamantly opposed to this idea. I had a speaking engagement out west, and took my family with me. We went to the Grand Canyon for a holiday. Each day I would call Neil, and we would talk about the progress at the table. He finally called me while we were staying in a hotel overlooking the Grand Canyon and he said, "Charlie, we will get an agreement if you will just let go of this issue of dues." And I said, "Neil, I'm standing at a window looking at a hell of a hole that was a product of steady erosion, and I think that's what you're doing. But we need to get this closed, so go ahead open up the canyon."

Anyhow, I recognized his ability and brought him to the provost office. It was created with the idea that we would share the presidency. This allowed me to continue as president to be directly involved in academics. But it went beyond that. The idea was that the senior officers of the institution would interact with each other rather than a series of vice presidents reporting to the president. I refused to draw a line organizational chart—instead I drew a series of circles. Carol accused me of having an anal fixation, but a circle was descriptive of what I was trying to accomplish.

SC: Holistic. [laughs]

CP: [laughs] Yes, that is the word I used repeatedly. But the idea was that they needed to talk to each other, not just to me. I really became convinced of the importance of that. It's a Likert model of organizational behavior. We began a pattern of meeting daily for a half hour. If the dean of students said, "We've got this problem, and I'd like you all to be aware of it," or if the vice president for administration said, "This was coming up with the AFSCME [American Federation of State, County and Municipal Employees] union," or something or other, there was a sense that they were talking not to me as president, but they were talking to each other. And Neil as provost was very much a part of that conversation.

I think it contributed to our ability to change the climate because one of the things I learned was a bit of a surprise—not completely a surprise, I sensed it from my visits—is that the pattern of open budget hearings with zero sum results had created an animosity that carried over even to the senior officers in the institution. This wasn't overt behavior— well, there was some—a kind of picking at each other, actually they were making war on each other. You can't have a university when it is being pulled apart. I hoped, and I think, our senior administrator model did contribute to a holistic scheme that later transferred into a planning model.

In 1978, how I don't really know, the *Wall Street Journal* heard of this, and they sent a reporter down to Athens. He spent two days wandering around campus, talking to people. I was very uneasy. We had gotten plenty of bad press in the *Plain Dealer* and elsewhere, and reporters tend to talk to each other, so I wasn't quite sure what was going to come out of this. But the piece that was published on the front page of the *Wall Street Journal* that year was absolutely a boost for the whole institution. It described and praised this holistic model of organization and of planning.

SC: One of the things that impressed me as a younger, moving into mid-career, member of the faculty, was that group of your chief administrators called the "11:30 Group." They didn't have a fancy title. They weren't called the senior leadership or senior administrators—

CP: Yes.

SC: they were the 11:30 Group. And I always admired the understanding that if one of them couldn't make a meeting; they didn't send a representative.

CP: That's right.

SC: The conversation was meant to be between the four or five of them—

CP: Yes.

SC: and you, and not as some reporting opportunity. So, I was always impressed with that as a way of making an administration work and cooperate.

CP: Well, I think it worked, and it worked through a succession of provosts, mostly because of the quality of the people. When Jim Bruning took
over from Neil, the University didn't miss a beat. When Dave Stewart
became provost, the organization again didn't miss a beat. And they were
very different people, different backgrounds. One of the nice things that
came to me in the year I retired is that 11:30 Group and their wives or
husbands gathered out in the Hocking Hills for a dinner, just a private
dinner with this group. In the course of the evening, they presented me
with a painting that they had commissioned. The painting, by Professor
[Gary] Pettigrew, is the back side of Cutler Hall. The side you don't see
very often; it is looking at Cutler toward where my office was, from the
Library side. And the clock on the steeple is stopped at 11:30. They had
asked Professor Pettigrew to do the painting with the clock stopped at
that moment.

　　　The desk in my office was a round table inherited from John Baker.
Interestingly, I had from time to time tried to convince the group that
maybe this was not a good use of their time, that maybe we ought to go
to weekly meetings rather than daily meetings. I was concerned that it
did cut into everybody's day; as they hustled at 11:30 to be down there. We
ended at noon, or very close to noon every day. If we didn't get it done
in that time, we didn't get it done that day. But everyone was so strongly
convinced that this helped them do their work, and that it was important
to them, they vetoed the change.

SC: One of the other things that was a phenomenon at Ohio University
was that the '60s didn't seem to end here until late into the '70s. We faced
a semiannual disturbance on Court Street where the kids felt that it was
their prerogative to take the street, which was a holdover from antiwar
protests in the sixties. Attempts were made to try to corral that problem
because it was intimately linked with the notion of Ohio University as a
party school. A party school with a first-rate School of Journalism, so that
any time a party overflowed into the streets, it was immediately on the
wire across the country because you had eight hundred stringers in the
School of Journalism.

CP: Yes, we had more stringers per hundred population than in any other place in the country. The single most important factor in ending that pattern was we had a change in the chief of police. Rather than the local police assuming that they were going to show students who were in control by getting them off the street and keeping them off the street, the police began to bend a little.

It followed one year's disturbance, when, sadly, they were firing rubber bullets at the students, and one of the rubber bullets struck and destroyed the eye of an international student. It was beginning to get ugly. It was confrontational. Students reveled in that. We tried to meet with bar owners, with city government, but nothing materially changed until the new police chief—

SC: Ted Jones?

CP: Ted Jones came to the conclusion that maybe if they could bend a little—let them have the street—then somehow the whole difference of the student perspective: "We're gonna show the police. Oh, we've got the street!" would change when the police response was, "You want the street, take the street." Then it wasn't nearly so much fun.

I can remember when you, Sam Crowl, were chair of the Faculty Senate. We were trying to do everything that we could to quiet this all down, and the police had specifically asked that I not come uptown during the crowded hours because I stuck out like a lightning rod. But it was so tempting. It was so hard to sit listening to all the sounds and fretting over a disaster just aching to happen. You had been patrolling the streets— well, actually, two stories involving you.

I went off to Culver, Indiana, to speak at the anniversary of the Memorial Chapel of Culver Military Academy. At five o'clock on a Sunday morning, a call from the city police came, "We have a prisoner who claims he is the chairman of the Faculty Senate and that he was trying to end the disturbance and was not a part of the disturbance." I said, "Describe him." And they described a bearded man without much hair on top of his head. I said, "That's the chair of the Faculty Senate you've got in jail," and they turned you loose.

I remember another year when you came to the house as the disturbance was beginning to break up. We went out together to see, we hoped,
the end of a long evening. We were at the top of Jeff [Jefferson] Hill. The
students had been throwing rocks at all the streetlights and managed to
knock most of them out. Suddenly we found that you and I were in the
dark out in front of the police lines as they tried to move the students
back down Jeff Hill. We looked around and realized that we were un-
wisely out front. You hollered to the students, who were crouched down
below, "Don't throw rocks, it's President Ping and Professor Crowl!"
Whoom! Incoming! [laughs] And we beat our way back up the hill and
went to my house and had a drink at four o'clock in the morning or whatever time it was.

SC: Our lucky day. [laughs] Back home in one piece.

CP: Yes.

SC: Well, one had the sense that there was some way to be helpful, and
        I'm afraid we probably weren't helpful but, I still thought—

CP: Yes.

SC: it was a good idea to show the flag that there were adults, in the
        neighborhood. Yes, those were exciting and sometimes dangerous times.
        Finally, it settled down. It is something today that has turned into
        another element of what makes Athens, Athens, the Athens known
        beyond the boundaries of Southeastern Ohio. We helped create a sanc-
        tioned Halloween.

CP: [laughs]

SC: A way of being good-spirited. We understand that a party can be
        important, and it can also be done in the right way, and I'm afraid we
        started it—

CP: Yes, actually Carol Harter started it when she was dean of students as a way of building town and campus relationships. We had a children's costume parade and prizes in the evening. We had a big cake on the steps of the Courthouse, and the Marching 110 came down the street at midnight. That was the first year or two. The first year there were a few thousand, mostly our own students, and everybody had a good time. The next year, it was a little bigger, and the year after that it was bigger still, and pretty soon it wasn't possible for the Marching 110—

SC: To get on the street.

CP: That's right, or for anyone else, including fire trucks and emergency vehicles. And it has been ever since a disaster waiting to happen. We have been fortunate that a disaster has not happened. Joking, to student groups, I offered to send buses to any other campus that they wanted to go to. I said I would rent buses for the Miami students to go to Ohio State, or wherever they wanted at Halloween. No one took me up.

SC: Once you had a sense of having stabilized the situation both financially and humanly, and the notion of the University being an effective community began to sink in, what did you turn your attention to as a way of accomplishing the broader academic goals that you had in mind for the University?

CP: Well, one of the key goals was to try to define what might be a core or general educational program for the University. We submitted a proposal to a foundation which had been sponsoring summer workshops in Colorado Springs for faculty teams to work on a self-identified problem. Once we had been selected to participate, a team, mostly faculty, was asked to address the problem and prepare a proposal for the campus. And the year before, we had commissioned a set of background papers on a whole series of issues in curriculum reform. These were distributed and discussed widely. The team included a dean, Dean [William] Dorrill of the College of Arts and Sciences, you were a faculty member on that team, and Nick Dinos was from engineering, and several others. It was broadly representative of the colleges. The team spent an extended period of time in Colorado Springs meeting and talking. They came back with a proposal that was submitted to the Faculty Senate. After a seemingly endless debate, it was adopted by the Faculty Senate. The program described a three-tier structure of general education.

The Tier structure stayed in place for what's typically the life span, twenty years, of a general education program. The first Tier identified basic learning skills; the second Tier described a breadth of education. The third Tier, which was really the unique part of the program, was designed to be interdisciplinary, an experience for seniors as a capstone. We had some outside funding that you and others managed to get that allowed us to convene workshops in the following summers to plan and develop new interdisciplinary courses. We had some really quite substantive and striking courses. I remember one involved a history professor and a physics professor dealing with issues of war and peace, and nuclear deterrence, as a focus. There were a lot of others. And I think the failure to find funds to sustain those summer workshops—I don't think this kind of thing can last very long if it's not continually renewed by faculty working together—spelled the end of Tier III. We simply didn't have the wherewithal to do it.

SC: The position papers that you talked about led to the second phase in terms of what we might do about core requirements—because there were none: they had been disbanded in the late '60s, as had happened on many campuses. But it really takes us back to strategic planning, to something else that you introduced to the campus. Those were not exactly words that the faculty had grown up with—

CP: [laughs]

SC: as a part of their educational experience. This notion of having a planning process largely driven by intellectual ideas. Could you talk a bit about that?

CP: Yes. This had been a part of what I am. I'm a Hegelian, and I wanted to look to the end to determine where we were going. It was that planning process that attracted the *Wall Street Journal* to campus. When I first began to talk about the planning process on campus, there was an almost audible groan because there had been a steady succession of efforts at planning that seemed to have very few consequences. One of the keys to successful planning is that it has consequences, cash value. That is, that it translates into something in the way of support.

We organized the campus into a grouping of some sixteen or eighteen planning units. The physical plant was a planning unit, each of the colleges was a separate planning unit, and so on. Then we set up a University Planning Advisory Council that consisted of the Executive Committee of the Faculty Senate, three students, a handful of other appointments—a dean and so forth.

This group of people was charged with the task of trying to look to the good of the institution as a whole. We set aside money for them to be able to fund ideas, even if it meant withdrawing money from units; all this to allow the group to make recommendations that had consequences. The provost chaired the group as part of the president's presence, so there was nothing that happened at UPAC that came as a surprise when they reported to me.

It was ultimately a report that went to the trustees as a recommendation that I was making to the trustees as president. UPAC, I think, understood right from the start that if I was not going to accept one of their recommendations I would at least meet with them, and explain, and argue if need be, and allow them the opportunity to convince me. Usually in the first session each fall of UPAC, I would go and say, "Now's the time to take off your engineering hat, physical plant hat, and so forth, and put on your university hat. That's what you're here for." Everyone would serve three-year terms, and they would rotate off. This meant the University was building, over time, a core of people who understood something about the institutional budget and about institutional planning—

SC: And about institutional needs.

CP: Yes.

SC: And the areas that you imagined they were interested in.

CP: Exactly. Yes. I think one of the things that undoubtedly gave it a boost was that we had private funds as a result of a very successful 1804 Campaign. A very sizable gift from [C.] Paul Stocker was unrestricted; we called the pool the 1804 Fund and divided the income from the endowment evenly between undergraduate instruction and research. Because we are a university, we have a commitment, a serious commitment, to both undergraduate education and graduate education and research.

Two of the things that I am proud of during the years that I was president were we achieved the formal stature of being recognized as a research university, and secondly, under Hwa-Wei Lee's leadership, the Library was recognized as one of 118 or so research libraries in North America.

One of the interesting sidelights, on the Library's recognition, was that Hwa-Wei Lee did such a good job of introducing automation, before it was commonplace in most university libraries. With his know-how and technology orientation, our application was acceptable in every area except the number of staff the Library had. The Association of Research Libraries criticized us; and we kept replying, "But we're doing the job. We're adding volumes to the Library; we're circulating the books. We are, in fact, doing all of the things that supposedly are measures of a functioning research university library and we're doing it with fewer people. Why should you penalize us for that?" [laughs] Finally, we won the argument.

But I think that the planning did, in fact, gain acceptance because people saw the recommendation beginning to make a difference. You know, planning is not a process that has as its outcome some recommendations on a shelf. It's a process that feeds into the budget process, or it has no value whatsoever, except, perhaps, as an exercise.

SC: One of the things that universities like to talk about doing, but don't always do so well, is collaboration and interdisciplinary work. You found ways in your administration to reward that kind of work.

Under the direction and guidance of Dean of Libraries Dr. Hwa-Wei Lee, pictured in 1983, the Ohio University Libraries grew in size and reputation and earned recognition as a world-class research institution when it joined the ranks of the prestigious Association of Research Libraries in 1996.

What were some of the ideas, or some of the processes that you employed in order to get units, academic units in particular, thinking together about projects?

CP: Well, we tried to use interdisciplinary efforts as one of the keys to awarding the 1804 grants. When it was possible for groups from various disciplines to collaborate in research projects, they could find money to help them do it. They were modest funds, seed money, but they were enough to make a difference. For example, Tom Wagner was on the threshold of major breakthroughs, but he needed a recombinant DNA laboratory. He submitted one of the proposals that came through the process of review and landed on my desk. I remember reading it, picking up the phone, and saying, "It's an intriguing idea, but I still don't understand; what in the world is a recombinant DNA laboratory, what does it do, and why is it important?" He tried to explain, and I think I understood a little bit. But out of that modest beginning came a marvelous breakthrough. He developed the ability to move a gene from one species of mammal to another. This story of his research results made the front page of newspapers from Rome to London to San Diego.

SC: An early example of the collaboration between chemistry and biology.

CP: Yes. With the infusion of a little support to help make it happen. I think the effort to develop the Tier III courses was a second clear strategy to encourage and to support interdisciplinary work.

SC: Later on, were you not also successful in moving such ideas statewide during the [Governor Richard] Celeste administration? Didn't the Celeste administration pick up on some funding notions that we had been working with here that made larger state grants available for such interdisciplinary efforts?

CP: Well, I have worked with a series of governors. Each was his own person; each was very different. But Governor Celeste was the one who was most willing to listen to an idea and then to take it and to run with it. I think that his Program of Excellence, with everyone competing for state funding for excellence, reflected some of our conversations, the pieces that were put together in Governor Celeste's package of funding for excellence had a symbiotic interaction in ways that no other state's program had. There was everything from support for undergraduate programs to research professorships, all involving a whole set of qualitative judgments. The state was putting money behind those qualitative judgments. For example, after Tom's wonderful breakthrough, Governor Celeste and others, as well as the legislature, were persuaded to give us the first biotechnology center here in Athens. And it was the Edison Biotech Center [Edison Biotechnology Institute]. That raised some eyebrows because, "Why would it go to Athens?" We got several endowed eminent scholar positions, one of which is the Goll-Ohio Eminent Scholar, which Professor

[John] Kopchick fills today. And he has had a tremendous impact. He worked closely with Tom, and a whole core of people, including some who broke off to form DHI [Diagnostics Hybrid Inc.]. It is a wonderful story. But Kopchick's discovery of a chemical means to address a medical problem—I'm over my head—finally got patented, and it was licensed to a pharmaceutical company. It now brings in something like six million dollars a year to Ohio University's operating budget.

SC: I think we have one of the highest returns on those patents of any university in the state, if not in the nation.

CP: Well, certainly among public universities in the state of Ohio, we're in a class all by ourself.

SC: You mentioned Kopchick, and you mentioned Tom Wagner. Can you mention a few other faculty members who benefited from the planning process and the way in which additional monies allowed them to make their ideas a reality?

CP: Well, I think one of the good illustrations is John Gaddis and the Contemporary History Institute. Now John took the idea and went outside and found funding—

SC: The MacArthur Foundation.

CP: He enlisted the Baker family in the effort. I think of the film program and David Thomas and a whole set of people in that program, visual communication and Terry Eiler and colleagues. I can't begin to identify how many people did, in fact, develop centers of excellence within the life of the University, aided in many cases by a little boost in funding from the 1804 grant.

SC: One of the areas that you mentioned early on, when talking about elements that were already alive in the Ohio University community that might have been surprising, was its international community. And that's certainly something that you built upon—

CP: Yes.

SC: in your time as president. Do you want to talk a bit about what your own sense was of the importance of the University being involved in the broader, larger world, and then some of the areas in the University that were particularly effective in being involved in international education?

CP: Well, first of all you started with a heritage—John Cady and the Southeast Asian Studies Center. That, in part, led to the involvement of the business college in Malaysia for more than twenty years. The business college entered into agreements with the Malaysian government to staff a Malaysia program for the people of that land leading first to the BBA degree and after to the MBA. Prime Minister Mahathir [Mohamad] was so impressed by the contribution that these programs were making to that country that he, in turn, was willing to support the funding of an endowed chair to bring Malaysian faculty members here, which of course, enhanced the Southeast Asia Studies.

We did a couple of things. One was to ensure that every project overseas had as its core staff regular faculty from here, not people hired just to do the project. And secondly, there was a conscious effort to build a relationship, a relationship, for example, that would translate in several cases into library materials. The Malaysian government early on identified the Alden Library as a depository for all official government documents. Botswana followed suit.

Then, we were very active in seeking overseas projects, funded by USAID [United States Agency for International Development], in education and in health—a whole series of areas—but principally education. This goes back long before I was here to projects begun under John Baker, and Vern Alden, in Nigeria and in Kenya. I personally got involved in some of these projects later. I tried to stay close to the faculty who were there and to visit them from time to time. As a result I was invited to

Presentation of a gift to the Libraries from the Malaysian government in 1988: (*left to right*) Dr. Felix Gagliano, Dr. Richard McGinn, Dr. Charles Ping, Dr. Abdullah Hassan (Tun Abdul Razak Chair), and Dr. Hwa-Wei Lee.

participate in the formal convocation that proclaimed an independent University of Botswana. Among the SADC [Southern African Development Community] countries, the University of Botswana is a model of what the university in a developing country should be. Initially it was three buildings on a dusty field, and our convocation was open air, fortunately with a sun shield over the platform.

You know when I came to Ohio University the largest pool of international students at that time was from Nigeria. Why? Because we had had successful projects in Nigeria. Then the bottom fell out of the Nigerian economy with the collapse of oil prices. Suddenly, we had a core of a hundred or more Nigerian students stranded with no support coming. The counsel general for Nigeria was one of our graduates; and he and the ambassador said, "We're sorry, but we don't have any hard currency to send." Bank One agreed to loans underwritten by the Ohio University Foundation for all the Nigerian students who needed it. The

President Ping meeting with visitors from Bangkok University in the president's office, 1984; President Charoen Kanthawongs (*second from left*) and Vice President Thanu Kulachol flank President Ping.

students assumed an obligation that when they got back home and were gainfully employed they would pay back the loans. I don't carry in my head the number, but I do know every single dollar was paid back.

Within a few years, we had 350 Malaysian students on campus. Malaysia was now the largest sender of students. I sat with the Malaysian ambassador, whose son happened to be a student here, and said, "I think that this is a mistake to concentrate so many of your students on two or three campuses in the U.S.," which is what they had done. They create their own little village, and we don't have fruitful interaction. Now Malaysia sends students all over the United States.

We worked with Malaysia in the process of developing higher education—they only had one university when we first went to Malaysia —now they have eight or so. Our role was to assist them in the early years in developing faculty. They sent graduate students here; the graduates secured a place for us in the life of Malaysia. In fact, the largest alumni dinner I ever went to was in Kuala Lumpur. We had over a thousand alumni at the dinner. On another occasion, the King of Malaysia showed up for an Ohio University alumni affair.

In more recent years, of course, the largest pool of students has been Chinese. It was a major event when the Chinese Education Delegation visited Ohio University in 1978. We built on Dean Dorrill's encouragement and help—he was the dean of the College of Arts and Sciences and a Chinese scholar; he had lots of good ties to the State Department. This was the first opening of China to US education, and Ohio University was the only campus in the Midwest where they made an official visit.

SC: Stanford, Harvard, and here.

CP: Yes, well, I think they stopped at Cal Tech and a couple of other places along the way. But it was West Coast—East Coast, and then the Ohio University airport or "Albany international." They spent the day on the campus. It was a delegation of intellectuals, university presidents, and party officials. They were led by the then president of Beijing University, a physicist by training, who had been trained at Cal Tech.

The University got some very good national coverage out of that visit. But we also were among the first campuses to receive Chinese students because that's what it represented—an opening. The first few years, the only Chinese students we got were thirty- and forty-year-old faculty who had been sent off to work in the rice paddies and the coal mines because intellectuals were suspect.

SC: Mao's Cultural Revolution.

CP: The Cultural Revolution. Now they were back on campus, and they had been out of touch with their disciplines for years and years. They wanted to work in a laboratory, or to do research that would get them back in touch with what had gone on. So, very few degrees were granted. Then gradually, we began to get graduate students because the Chinese universities were trying to stock their universities. Where we had strength, for example, biochemistry, Ohio attracted some wonderful graduate stu-

President Ping and Professor of Chemistry James Tong at a meeting of the Hong Kong Chapter of the Ohio University Alumni Association, 1987. Daniel Shao, president of the chapter and long-serving trustee of the Ohio University Foundation, is second from the right in the back row.

dents here and, around the campus, other centers of excellence brought people destined to be faculty; and a great many Chinese librarians came to study the operations of Alden Library.

While I was in Beijing at a leading science university there, my host was the vice president for research. As we were going around the campus, and conversation lent itself to this kind of remark, I thanked him for the quality of the graduate students that they had sent. I talked about the young woman who had come to Tom Wagner's lab, she was one of the perfectors for the technology for the transfer of genes; I identified a couple of others. He was beaming from ear to ear because one of the students at Ohio had been his student.

The vice president explained, "President Ping, you have to understand" —my numbers are all wrong—"but there are millions of Chinese students

President Ping walks with the president of Peking University, Zhou Peiyuan, on the College Green during the Chinese Education Delegation's visit to the Athens campus, 1978.

who stand the university exams. The government sends us the top 5,000 from which we pick the top 2,000 that we want in our entering class. And, then from that 2,000, we pick the hundred or so that we will send abroad for graduate study. What you're talking about is a product of that selection." [laughs] Anyhow, the flow of Chinese students has continued, and that's true across the country. China is sending more students than any other country to study in the United States.

One of the things that began to strengthen during this period was our own effort to send our students abroad. That's still well below what it ought to be, true, but there are significant numbers of Ohio University students now studying abroad, many in Ohio University programs abroad. This is critical to the internationalization of a university.

SC: Yes, because it's got to be a two-way street.

CP: Sure.

SC: Sometime in the mid-'80s, I was having a conversation with a professor who had just come here from a professorship at Penn State, and I said, "You've been here a year: what do you see as the similarities and differences between the two campuses?" And he said, "Well, obviously Penn State is bigger, but the geographic area is very similar. What strikes me most is that Penn State has about the same number of international students as Ohio University, but you would never know that they were there. But Ohio University is very proud of its international students, and goes a long way to remind the campus that they're amongst us." As we're approaching it this May—was International Week one of your ideas that came up during your administration?

CP: It came up. I don't think it was my idea. [Dean of Students] Joel Rudy deserves credit for the closing of Court Street and the International Fair and for many other valuable additions to student life.

SC: The flags leading up to Cutler Hall—

CP: as well as the use of the flags on ceremonial occasions.

SC: The fact that they hang from the rafters of the Convocation Center—

CP: Yes.

SC: every time that you are in watching a basketball game or any other event in there—

CP: or commencement—

SC: is a reminder of the University's international commitment.

CP: Yes.

SC: Was that an idea of yours?

CP: Oh, I think Joel Rudy again deserves credit, but it was clearly part of the very real commitment of the institution to the internationalization of the University.

SC: You mentioned, particularly about international education, two of your predecessors, John Baker and Vern Alden. There is a remarkable history between the three of you, three men who had presidencies at Ohio University between 1945 and 1994, and who have maintained involvement with the University throughout their lives. Could you talk a bit about the sort of way in which you saw Baker, as a mentor, or Alden as a mentor, and a colleague?

CP: Well, I told you the story about the search committee and the meeting in Vern's office and the expression of deep feeling about their experience that Marion and Vern had. John Baker was just the same way. I was privileged to have a friendship with Vern and Marion and with John and his wife, Elizabeth, and with the Baker children, three women I have cherished knowing.

In 1975, John was well on in years, but he was destined to live for another quarter of a century, and I made it a practice every summer that I taught in the summer program at Harvard to go out on Cape Cod, to the Monomoy Weekend. Claire and I usually stayed with the Bakers, or with one of the daughters in Chatham.

I remember well my first visit. I had been named president, but was not yet on campus. I drove out on Cape Cod to meet the Bakers. They had this old house, which used to be an old sea captain's lodging in the harbor there at Chatham. It is a lovely sprawling house on a hill over-looking the bay. There I met John and Elizabeth for the first time. John immediately had some things that he wanted to tell me, so he said, "Come on, let's go out on the front lawn." We sat side by side in lawn chairs, and we started talking. He wanted to tell me things that concerned him and—

SC: He always had an agenda—

CP: Yes, he did. We had been talking only a few minutes when Elizabeth came out, pulled up a chair, sat down beside us. She had a few things she wanted to talk about, and she changed the subject from what John wanted. She wanted to talk about the theater program and so forth. I was sort of a ping-pong ball going back and forth. John said, "Maybe we'd be more comfortable on the other side of the house." He got up, walked around the house and put the chair down on the other side of the house, I think anticipating that Elizabeth wouldn't join us. But she did. We kept on with this kind of dialogue.

One of John's great contributions to the University was to recog-nize, in 1945, that there was no reason, as he put it—I think I'm quoting; if not, I'm paraphrasing—"There's no reason why a good public univer-sity shouldn't have private support, just as private universities do." He proposed to the trustees that the Ohio University Fund be created to channel dollars into the private funding effort, but the chairman of the board, and other members of the board, opposed the idea. After all, they paid taxes, and taxes supported the University. You couldn't double tax, or ask people who are already paying for the University to pay for it again. Well, John had a persistent way about him, and before long, he had incorporated the Ohio University Fund.

Ohio was one of the earliest public universities to have an organized effort to build private support. I think it was—when I came on—something that was unrealized in its potential, but it was there, and the fact that this tradition was already in place opened up possibilities. We had a total endowment of about a million and a half, but we had good people who organized it. If you're going to have a successful effort, you have to have volunteers to do it through a foundation board.

John always said that when somebody told him his most lasting legacy might be the Ohio University Fund, his feelings were hurt. He said that he thought his lasting legacies were the dimensions of the academic program, or the PhDs that had been started, not the fund. But he conceded that they may have been right.

SC: What was the endowment when you left office?

CP: Oh, I don't know. We had two successful campaigns. The 1804 Campaign in 1978, which was launched with a very auspicious meeting of all three of the boards: the board of trustees, the foundation board, and the alumni board. We met in a state park—

SC: Salt Fork.

CP: Salt Fork, thank you. After a great deal of discussion—there had already been a feasibility study. It had been shelved because the times were not right for a campaign. The three boards unanimously approved the idea of launching a national campaign, really the first in the history of the institution, although John had a sesquicentennial program to raise scholarship dollars. These three boards with enthusiasm embraced the idea. I said, "The only problem is you can't run a campaign without money to run it. We don't have any money to start it."

We took a break, and Paul and Beth Stocker put their heads together. When we reconvened, Paul Stocker said, "I'll put up the money for the start of the campaign." We were off and running. When we publicly launched the campaign sometime after this meeting at Salt Fork, Paul had died, and his will had been probated, and we were left with the odd launching of what the professional advisors told us would reach a $24 million campaign with about $23 million already in hand. Now that's a happy problem to have. So the campaign went on well beyond the goal.

Then in the late 1980s, we launched a second campaign, the Third Century Campaign. The professional counsel that we had at the time said, "You might raise $70 million, but it would take a lot of hard work." The foundation board and I thoroughly agreed, and said, "Let's set the sights high enough to be aspirational." So the goal was $100 million, and we raised about $130 million. I think that it has provided some significant margin of difference in the life of the University.

To go back to Paul Stocker: Paul had a particular interest in the engineering college. He had wanted to start an endowed chair in electrical engineering. In a phone conversation he said, "I'll give you fifty thousand dollars a year to fund the chair." Back then that was the kind of money it took to attract a first-rate person. I said, "Paul, if you do that then when you're gone we don't have an endowment that will support it. What we've got to do is have an endowment to support the position." Paul said, "Well, maybe you better come up and talk with me." I said, "Sure."

So we spent the best part of a day talking about the University and its future, and the engineering college and its future. He finally asked me a question, "All right, Charlie, if you could identify one thing that would make the greatest difference in the College of Engineering what would it be?" I thought for a minute. The first general college faculty meeting that I had had on campus was with the engineering faculty. They beat me up badly for two hours about the lack of funding for engineering. I said, "Paul, I think the institution will manage to scrape together the dollars to keep the faculty on board, but what's happened over the past decade is that the College of Engineering has been starved for equipment, and starved for seed money to start research. If you're going to have an

Portrait of C. Paul and Beth K. Stocker, ca. 1974.

engineering college, instrumentation has to be a part of its basic requirement. We've gone a decade with almost no money to build that instrumentation. So I think the answer to your question is an endowment that would in fact fund equipment and advanced research." Then he asked me, "Well, how about the University as a whole? What would you say is the single most important thing?" I said, "Well, Paul, if we had some unrestricted dollars then we could use the income to push the campus in particular directions."

I didn't realize it at the time, but what I was actually doing was writing the language of a codicil to his will. When the estate was probated, he divided his estate in half: half going to the College of Engineering to support the purchase of equipment and advanced research, and half of it coming as an endowed unrestricted discretionary endowment to be determined by the University.

That unrestricted money is the hardest money in the world to raise. Most donors give to things that interest them, and here was Paul's blessing, giving to the University and letting the University define its use. As he said to me, "You know, I can't define what the University's needs are in twenty, or a hundred years from now, any more than you can." And that was in his will. So, that's the genesis of the 1804 Fund.

SC: What an interesting group of people. You already mentioned Ed Kennedy, and now you've talked about the Stockers. The Russes [Fritz J. and Dolores H. Russ] would be—

CP: Yes.

SC: in there as a very special and generous couple. And, of course the Konnekers [Wilfred and Ann Lee Konneker], all people who have probably graduated from the University sometime between the '20s and the '50s, who have been remarkably successful in their careers and remain remarkably loyal to the University. Not only in giving their treasure, but also their time.

CP: Yes. And this includes Vern Alden and for years, John Baker.

SC: They worked on all these campaigns, they solicited others, and they come back two or three or four times a year to meetings—

CP: Yes.

SC: and it's still going on. Remarkable.

CP: Well, Will Konneker is at the head of that list for so many reasons. I remember when the University was searching for an alumni facility. We looked at George Weckman's house next to the president's residence; we wanted something around campus. The Alumni Association was housed at that time in a couple of offices in Lindley Hall; their offices were way in the back. You had to want to get there to find the Alumni Association offices. Will and Ann Lee stepped into the conversation and said, "We will purchase the Grosvenor house from its present owner. We'll refurbish and restore it to its former grandeur, and then turn it over to the University as the Alumni House." If you can picture what an alumni house should look like for this campus, that's the Grosvenor House. Ann Lee and my wife, Claire, and a number of other people worked and worked to identify proper interior decoration and the pieces that would go inside the house.

When the faculty committee from arts and sciences brought back a response to my proposal that we establish a research park, the committee very wisely reported that Athens is not a place for a research park, there is not enough corporate presence in the area to make it feasible. What we really need is an "Innovation Center," something that might nurture businesses, take ideas, take discoveries, and turn them into economic activity. I saw the sensibleness of the recommendation. The only problem was that we didn't have anybody to lead the effort.

Will Konneker could act as a role model. He and Ann Lee had started in their basement or garage a nuclear diagnostic company that grew to be a very, very, very successful enterprise. He had taken science and his research, and translated it into economic activity. When they sold their business, the new owner named Will the international vice-president, and he built on ideas that came from elsewhere.

Will was quick to agree to lead the idea on campus. He would give us one week a month for an indefinite period of time to help start the Innovation Center. We put him in a couple of offices in an abandoned building off of President Street, and he set to work. He went around to the faculty and said, "Share your ideas. Look at them in terms of their potential. We're in an economically impoverished region. We need new discoveries, new ideas to turn into businesses." The faculty really didn't think this way at all.

SC: No.

CP: It took a lot of encouragement. We didn't have a patent office, which is a central part of this kind of process. Without Will Konneker, we wouldn't have an Innovation Center. For the next two years, he gave a week a month: he made the rounds, he worked with ideas, and he counseled people who had ideas, and patiently helped them understand how they could start businesses. The first year, I paid him a dollar a year. He did so well in that first year that I doubled his salary in the second year to two dollars. He loves this University. He was on the search committee when they were looking for a president. He was one of the reasons that I came here, and he's been one of the reasons I stayed here.

SC: I think maybe we should stop here. We've been doing this at a steady clip. We'll pick up where we were, and we'll come back to Will.

CONVERSATION
with
SAM CROWL

May 19, 2011

SC: Charlie, when we stopped in the last session, we were right in the middle of your telling the wonderful story of Will Konneker's many contributions to the University, and we were right in the middle of the development of the Innovation Center and—

CP: Yes, yes.

SC: the key role he played there. Could you pick it up, or flesh it out for us?

CP: Well, everywhere that you turn on campus, you find the evidence of Will Konneker's commitment to the University. The Innovation Center, as I said, was an idea that needed someone to take it off of the paper and put it into practice, and Will did it. He tirelessly worked with faculty to get them to explore the economic potential and, I think, it has had a marked impact on the region. Probably the most dramatic impact really didn't unfold for some years because most of these efforts take years to develop. But out of the work that Tom Wagner, Joe Jollick, and others were doing, a group began to see the economic potential in this, and started a small effort that became Diagnostic Hybrids. At first they occupied some abandoned labs in the old chemistry building; gradually they turned it into a profitable business. A business that struggled for years and Will Konneker kept it afloat.

SC: Explain, for those who aren't up to speed on Diagnostic Hybrids, what exactly they were doing with Wagner's research.

CP: They had a whole series of responses that changed over time, but basically they were developing material to supply to hospital labs that could, in fact, use the material to diagnose a variety of things. Eventually, in twenty years, Diagnostic Hybrids became the largest supplier of cell and other culture materials for laboratories. It is a wonderful story.

Dave Scholl, who was the CEO of this small company, had been a graduate student. Finishing his PhD in biochemistry, he immediately, with Joe Jollick's help, turned his attention to this project. He gradually worked with a handful of others and Will Konneker to keep it all afloat. Will would come to my office late in the afternoon and say, "Charlie, that's the last one. I've signed my last promissory note; they're gonna have to pull their own weight." We talked for a while, and went over to the house to have a drink and pretty soon he'd say, "Well, maybe one more time."

Talk about a success story. In the last two or three years, the company was sold for over $130 million to a California firm that pledged that they would maintain production and research facilities here. It has built into the life of this region a whole host of jobs, employing over two hundred people. It's a business that is growing. And the return to the Ohio University Foundation is very significant, $35 million, because the foundation made an early investment in it. Will Konneker turned over all of his founder's stock to the foundation with the insistence that 80 percent be dedicated to the Cutler Scholars and 20 percent to the Kennedy Museum. Most of which we need to go back and talk about.

But let me go on a bit and talk about Will Konneker. Will was president of the Alumni Association when I first met him, and he served, therefore, on the presidential search committee. Will was one of that group of people whose deep sense of commitment to this place attracted me here and held me here for the rest of my career. Will chaired two national campaigns, both very successful—the 1804 Campaign and the Third Century Campaign. That's unheard of—one individual being willing to volunteer for two capital campaigns.

We traveled together. We had dinners all over the country to celebrate the success of the Third Century Campaign. He even traveled to Malaysia to talk with them about biotechnology and its promise.

I think that I mentioned the last time, when we were searching for something that would give a visibility to the Alumni Association, Will and Ann Lee stepped forward and said, "We'd like to purchase the Grosvenor house," a stately old home right in the middle of campus, "and restore it to its nineteenth-century grandeur." And they did.

SC: We are right to be reminded of the history of Ann Lee's contributions and her friendship with Claire because they really went to work in terms of decoration of the home and taking over that carriage house, which has become known as Claire Cottage, a small house behind the Grosvenor house.

CP: Yes, they were devoted. Ann Lee actually searched for just the right pieces. All the furniture on the first floor was authentic from that period. Claire and Ann Grover and a whole group worked hard with that committee to see the Grosvenor house restored to its nineteenth-century appearance. The carriage house was a little convoluted, but Will and Ann Lee wanted to buy it as a piece of the whole property.

The wife of a longtime member of the foundation board, then a widow, said, "Let me buy it." She wanted to redo it completely and live on the campus, and she tore out the interior and was busily ordering cabinets. She intended to deed the house to the University. But, she died, unfortunately, before the papers were signed. The house then became part of an estate, and we eventually bought the house because it was essential to the property. The work that was started was finished. Then much to my joy, when I retired, the board of trustees took formal action to the effect that the carriage house shall be known in perpetuity as Claire [Oates Ping] Cottage in grateful recognition of the service that Claire gave to the University over our nineteen years.

SC: We've talked about Will Konneker, and we've talked about Paul Stocker, and we've talked a bit about Fritz Russ, and we'll come back. But talking about Ann Lee and talking about Claire leads me to ask you to say a few words about other prominent women who have given their souls and their treasure to the University. I'm thinking about people like Leona Hughes and Jody Galbreath Phillips and someone who's not a graduate of Ohio University, Charlotte Eufinger, who has given her time endlessly. Talk a bit about their contributions.

CP: Well, the individuals you mentioned are in the forefront of a whole core of women. Leona Hughes was very special. She was with the alumni board for years, served as secretary, and made sure that things happened as they ought to happen. She organized an alumni group in Sarasota, and it was sort of a command performance. Every December in the Christmas season, Claire and I would go down to Sarasota and stay with Leona and make a circuit with Leona of alumni groups in the area. The start was this annual luncheon in Sarasota, well over one hundred typically attended, and then the tour would go on to other cities in Florida. Leona was a force in the alumni activity, and she ensured that medals of merit and other sorts of activity were tended to with care.

As we began to plan for and start the Cutler Scholars, she was quick to step in. She had a deep loyalty to her hometown, Oak Hill, a small town in this area of the state. So she insisted that she would establish four scholars, Cutler Scholars, one each year from Oak Hill. She also established some need-based scholarships for students coming from Oak Hill. If we had a few alumni as loyal and as generous as Leona things would move ahead rapidly.

SC: She was famous, I recall, for doing this with her own Cutler Scholars later on in life. I think she had been very active in her sorority, and when

President Ping, with Claire Ping in the background, speaking on the front steps of the Konneker Alumni Center at the 1981 dedication.

Leona Hughes, who began her long OHIO career as a freshman undergraduate in 1926, is pictured here with a group of female students on her eightieth birthday, 1989.

she would come back to campus she would meet the sorority girls for breakfast. She got up at a very early hour to confront a day that for her began before dawn—

CP: [laughs]

SC: and didn't end until after midnight often.

CP: Yes, that's very true. Actually, she had a 7:30 a.m. breakfast meeting with the Cutler Scholars and the need scholars. She would explain to them in very pointed terms that the scholarship they were awarded was not a gift, it was a loan, and they were expected to repay it. [laughs] Hooray for her.

Jody Phillips was the chair of the board of trustees the year that the trustees were searching for a president. So as I came to the point that I was serious, and they were serious, it was with Jody that I negotiated the terms of my appointment.

There's a side story. I first met with this group while I was at Harvard in the Advanced Management Program. And the trustees of the university that I was then serving had sent me to this three-month-long Advanced Management Program in part to get me out of the way of a presidential search on that campus because, I think, I don't know this, but I think a majority of them were clearly leaning toward my candidacy. Anyway, when the call from Ohio University came, I met with them in Vern's office; things progressed from there. Finally, after it began to appear that it was something that interested me, and that they were interested in me, I said, "We've got to face the fact I am simply not free to be a candidate. I think that I have an obligation. The board of the university I serve has paid the enormous fee for the Advanced Management Program, and they had given me a three-month leave."

Ed Kennedy stepped up to me and said, "Mr. Ping, if we decide you are the person, that's not an obstacle—we'll take care of it. Jody and I will take care of it." And, they did. They wrote checks to Central Michigan University to reimburse them. Jody was an enthusiast; she was generous with the Galbreath Darby Dan Farm and its lovely estate. She allowed us to use it as a kickoff site for campaigns and celebrations of athletic events like the night before the Ohio State football game. She loved athletics, as did her father, and she was very supportive of athletics.

Charlotte Eufinger was a special case. A Miami graduate, she sent two children to Ohio University. And an active Democrat, she was appointed by a Democratic governor—

SC: Dick Celeste.

CP: to the board of trustees, and Charlotte was dedicated and faithful as anyone could be. Her two children are following in her footsteps. She was, among other things, chairman of the board when the plans were accepted for the building of a student activities center, after the Student Senate in the name of the student body agreed to assume the bonded indebtedness payments. Then they turned around, much to my joy, and recommended to the trustees that it be named in my honor. And the trustees did.

SC: I understand that you are proud of overhearing a conversation among students where your name has become a verb. How did that happen?

CP: [laughs] Ping is a verb. It's an adjective. I was walking behind a group of students after teaching a class, and one of them said to the other, "Well, I gotta go Ping." [laughs]

SC: [laughs]

CP: I had a curious experience. You know, the then chairman of the Graduate Student Senate, Elliot Ratzman, was a philosophy student, and I had him in several classes. He decided he was going to launch a protest, in which he would force the board of trustees to name an academic building in my honor, rather than this recreational facility. I had a private conversation with him and said, "Back off." He was really trying to tweak the nose of the trustees, as he so often did. And he did back off. Elliot went on to do a PhD, from Princeton. He is a first-rate scholar and a fine, I suspect, teacher.

SC: Speak about some other people on the foundation board, or on the board of trustees, who were exemplary presences in your day—

CP: Yes.

SC: both in their general wisdom that they brought to their responsibilities and in the effort that they put into making Ohio University a better place.

CP: Well, we ran two campaigns with Jack Ellis as the key. He was our computer. He had every bit of knowledge, every item that we needed, but we also made extensive use of members of the foundation board. The people who stepped up were people like Bob Axline, who tirelessly came back and forth from Boston to Athens to work in the campaigns. He cochaired the Third Century Campaign with Will.

President Ping with Jody Galbreath Phillips at her retirement from the board of trustees, 1979.

Ed Kennedy was a sitting trustee of the University and the foundation when I arrived. He took a very active interest and was a solid advisor for the investments when we began to have funds to invest. Ed and his wife were fascinating people. He was a partner of Lehman Brothers, and he had, specifically, responsibility for energy investments. He thus sat on the boards of major oil companies and traveled frequently to the Southwest.

Ed developed a very strong interest in the art of the Navaho Indians particularly, but broadly in Indian art. Over the years, he collected what the national Textile Museum described in its brochure for the show of some of his collection in Washington as the world's leading collection of Navaho weaving. I remember well spending an afternoon in their home. He had a huge vault in their basement, because these things were immensely valuable. We spent the afternoon. He would unfold blanket after blanket and explain their significance. I knew nothing about Indian weavings or blankets, but it is an impressive collection. Over the years, he had given his wife a series of gifts, many of which were commissioned, beautiful pieces of jewelry. He gave his wife flatware and silverware—only it was gold—all handmade by American Indians.

In any case, I talked with Ed about this because he was now beginning to think about the ultimate disposition of his collection. He said, "Well, I want it somewhere where the collection will be used." We talked, and an obvious choice was to have the bulk of the collection go to the University of New Mexico. He said that he would send representative pieces from each genre to Ohio. Then politics reared its ugly head at the University of New Mexico—the governor sat as a member of the board of regents, and they hired and fired presidents, and there was much coming and going. Finally, one night after a dinner and meeting in our home in the midst of a campaign, Ed pulled me aside and said, "May I stay for a bit and talk?" I said, "Sure." When we were alone, he said, "I feel that I really cannot trust the University of New Mexico because of the intrusion of politics, and I wonder if Ohio University would be willing to accept the entire collection?" And of course [laughs] I said, "Yes, indeed. We would be honored and pleased."

As soon as he made this a formal commitment, I went up to the governor, Governor Celeste at the time, and said, "This is a magnificent collection, and we have no place to display it. We simply need funding in the Capital bill funding for a museum." And he was persuaded. I said, "And it's true that this collection will draw schoolchildren by the busload and draw collectors and people interested in Indian culture." It had a very strong draw when it was displayed at the Textile Museum in Washington. Governor Celeste saw fit to include a museum in the Capital bill. It was the first time any state money was put into a museum on a campus.

Gene Rinta, chairman of the foundation board during my early years, was a very able and active board member. Fritz Russ, Bob Axline, Ed Kennedy, Will Konneker, Leona Hughes, Alan Riedel, and a whole corps of people that stand out. Jack Ellis was the key to enlisting people and whatever success we had in development.

Claire Ping, President Ping, and Edwin Kennedy (at podium) during the inauguration of Charles Ping as OHIO's president, March 1976.

SC: Chuck Emrick—

CP: Chuck Emrick came on the scene later and took a very active interest. He was a man of ideas. In Cleveland, he was a person people turned to, to get something put together and done, and getting things done was his strong suit on the foundation during the years that he served as a trustee. He has been very helpful with his Cutler Scholars and the program as a whole.

       One of the important and dedicated trustees of both the University and the foundation was Ralph Schey. Another was Fritz Russ. I cherished the opportunity to work with both Fritz and Ralph.

SC: Dean Jeffers, head of Nationwide Insurance.

CP: Dean Jeffers, CEO of Nationwide, was a University trustee. He was one of the very best managers I have ever known, really relating to the people who made the operation work. He was appointed by the governor—I think Rhodes appointed him. You know, Governor Rhodes seldom asked presidents for input. He'd pull something out of the air, and he wouldn't say where it had come from. Well, in this case, Dean had felt for years that he ought to get active at his alma mater, but he was busy building Nationwide into a great insurance corporation. Rhodes learned of his interest and appointed him; he proved to be a very effective trustee. At a personal and professional level, he was a man who taught me a great deal. I served on the Nationwide board, and I'm sure he was instrumental in getting me there.

Whenever the University board was in session, we would

Director of Development Jack Ellis, 1975.

find some occasion to walk together and talk. One of his standard lines was that he would turn to me and say, "Charlie, never forget you are only one board meeting away from getting fired." And since I had no contract, and didn't want a contract, that was true. I would turn to him and say, "You must remember that, too," because I was on his board as well. [laughs]

One of the very remarkable things about Ohio University is the trustees. By law, and uniquely among Ohio institutions, a majority of the trustees must be graduates of the institution. Governor Rhodes was the only one who chafed at this requirement. Governor Celeste was far more responsive to campuses, and he had a feel for universities and was willing to consult with presidents. Though a Democrat, he gave me two or three of our very finest trustees: Jenny [Jeanette] Grasselli Brown, an active Republican; also, Ralph Schey, an active Republican; both appointed by a Democrat governor.

SC: Jenny Grasselli was another one of those names that deserve to be in the group that we mentioned earlier as having a profound impact on the University.

CP: Indeed. She volunteered, for example, to spend a year in an appointment where her goal was to nurture the research activities on campus. She, herself, is a world-renowned physical chemist with all sorts of honors and recognitions. She is a lovely, dedicated person. She too has been central to the development of the Cutler Scholars.

SC: Let me mention another name, actually an Athenian who went to the University, and then went out into the world and did a remarkable series of jobs and held a remarkable number of positions. I know that you were very taken with him and that's Steve Fuller.

CP: Yes. Steve Fuller graduated from Ohio, as you pointed out, and he was invited to stay on for a couple of years as an instructor in the business school. John Baker urged him to go on and do graduate work at Harvard; he did, and finally ended up with a doctorate in business administration from Harvard. Very soon after his graduation, Steve was appointed to the Harvard faculty; later he occupied a named chair. He was a great teacher.

   From there, he went to Southeast Asia, and in Manila started an institute for training of managerial leadership for the businesses of Asia. His name opened doors all over Southeast Asia: Thailand and Malaysia, the Philippines and Indonesia. Many of the leaders of the business community were in their roles because of the training of the Asian Management Institute.

   Steve then came back to the States and was a vice president of General Motors. His vision affected a number of things in the area of people management at General Motors. Then he went back to Harvard, again to teach in a named professorship. When the Harvard Business School got concerned about the issue of people like me, who one day was a philosophy professor and the next day was a college or university president with nothing in between but the passage of time, they started an Institute for Educational Management.

I was involved as one of the first students when it was foundation funded. In the business school, it was an eight-week management program with the best of the Harvard faculty teaching cases, just like the cases they taught in the Advanced Management Program. Their hope was that university presidents and senior officers would, in fact, gain greater understanding and skill. Steve taught in that program, and I also taught in that program for about twenty years.

Each summer I would go to Harvard and spend about a week teaching. Because Steve taught the class session before mine, I made it a point to go to his class in the hope that I might come to some better understanding of how to be a really good teacher. Steve was, by far, the most effective case study teacher I've ever seen. He could stand a class on its ear and have everybody involved.

Anyhow, he retired from Harvard, and Ralph Schey asked him to take up one of his companies. Ralph was directly responsible for World Book. And he did. Both Steve and Ralph were active as trustees of the Ohio University Foundation. When he decided to retire from World Book, having turned it around and moved it to a profitable position, he was persuaded—I helped to persuade him—to return to Athens, his boyhood home. He and his wife did move to Athens. They bought what had been the Gordon Bush home and restored it to its original grace and beauty. He spent a number of years teaching in our business school. I remember a day at the end of his first term on the faculty. I'm sitting in my office; Steve comes marching in, and he's got a sheaf of papers in his hands. He dumps them on my desk, and says, "All right, you persuaded me to come here. Here are the student evaluations. You ought to understand what they're saying." [laughs] I smiled, and I said, "I'm delighted you will let me look at them." I read through them, and the comments sections were usually, "I signed up for this course thinking it was a management course. I didn't realize it was Composition 101."

SC: [laughs]

CP: [laughs] Because anyone who turned in a paper to Steve Fuller better be good and sure that it was grammatically correct with some sense of style.

SC: Steve Fuller's experience mirrored a part of your Ohio University experience. That is, going back and forth between Athens and the world. It brings me back to a subject that we touched on in the last session, and it is something that we might explore a little more fully, and that is Ohio University and the world. One of the areas that we didn't talk about was our whole relationship with Japan and with the Chubu Institute. Can you talk a bit about how that developed and the remarkable sort of institutional ties that—

CP: Well, Chubu needed a link to an American university for several reasons. One, because they were seeking to move to a university status, and the Ministry of Education looked favorably on such a tie. Secondly, they needed a tie to an American university to help train and bring on board faculty with completed graduate programs. Chubu was an institute originally, when I first visited it, supported by a foundation with close family ties to the life of the institution. Professor [Tomoyasu] Tanaka of our physics department was instrumental in building the relationship of the two institutions and served as the official translator for a number of my speeches at Chubu.

Among other things, they had established a professorship that would bring to the Chubu campus each year an Ohio University faculty member, primarily in the basic sciences or in engineering. Every faculty member who went was treated with great deference and courtesy, and they came home with their families, usually, just aglow from the experience. I understand that grace and thoughtfulness, having given many speeches on the campus of Chubu and been graciously entertained by President [Kazuo] Yamada.

I remember well the first trip to Nagoya and to the campus of Chubu. President Yamada hosted a dinner in our honor. Claire was with

President Ping, along with faculty and staff of the Chubu Institute and Ohio University, surround President Kazuo Yamada for the presentation of an honorary degree awarded posthumously to his father, Kohei Miura, the founding president of what is now Chubu University, 1976. Ohio and Chubu are joined as sister universities, and many of the OHIO faculty in the picture served as visiting faculty at Chubu.

me, and we were to dedicate, the next day, a major academic building for the campus. It is a great honor to be entertained in someone's home in Japan, and we were pleased to be invited to the Yamada home. As we came in, President Yamada greeted us and said to me, "May we take your wife and dress her?" I didn't quite know what he meant, but I thought I didn't have much choice. She was willing, and so they took her upstairs and bound her in all the undergarments that go with it and fitted her in a magnificent Japanese kimono. She came downstairs a picture of beauty in this kimono. And then we went into the tea ceremony room.

President Yamada's mother was a master, which is a recognized status in Japan. The only problem was that there was no way I could sit as they were seated. They kept piling pillows up higher and higher, and I ruined the dignity of the whole thing by flopping on this great pile of pillows. We had a traditional Japanese tea ceremony, an experience of great dignity and beauty.

As we headed to dinner, President Yamada again pulled me aside and said, "We would be very honored if you would participate in the Shinto ceremony prior to the public dedication of the building." I had no idea what a Shinto ceremony was, or what my participation entailed. When I paused for a minute, not because I was hesitating, I just didn't know what to say, he said, "Please understand I am a Christian, and we are in a room with a Buddhist shrine; Shinto is part of the culture of Japan." I said, "Of course." We sat down to a grand dinner. Mrs. Yamada never sat down while we were being served. She supervised the serving of the meal, and his mother-in-law presided at the table. So, I was learning bit by bit a lot of things about Japanese culture.

Anyway, the next day we went to the room that was set aside for the Shinto ceremony. There were Shinto priests, and each college, each department, the dean or the chairman would walk to the center and bow before an altar. On the altar there were fish, and there was sake, and there was rice. And the Shinto priest was very much at the center. The leader of each group, in turn, would come forward, and when they would bow, everybody from that department or college would clap.

Now Claire and I towered over this group of faculty and were very obvious—she was the only woman present. When the time came, we went up and did our bit, but we had no one to clap for us, and so we went back to our seats in silence. Once the ceremony was completed, we went into the next room, and we ate all the food that was on the altar and drank all the sake. President Yamada explained to me what we were doing: We were saying to the land how grateful we were for its surrender of its space to our building and our hope for a blessing and favorable return. In honor of this, we ate the fruit of the sea and the land. It was a remarkable experience.

When we celebrated our 175th anniversary, President Yamada came with an extraordinary gift to Ohio University—so like him—he gave in the name of his university 175 flowering Japanese cherry trees that grace the campus to this day, and to our joy, they bloom in the spring. Plus, an endowment to keep pace with the age of the institution, by the planting of additional cherry trees. There is a plaque marking the site where we dedicated those cherry trees. He was an able president, and he saw the maturing of Chubu to university status. We became very close friends.

One of the moments that I remember well occurred during one of his visits in a fall. I asked President Yamada and his party to join Claire and me in the president's box, which was a kind of chicken coop at the top of the stadium, at the time, for the football game, and he came. While we were seated there, without planning it, every faculty member who was in the stands, learning of his presence, would come with his family to visit. The smile on his face and the smile on their faces and their children spoke wonders about how rich this relationship had become.

Generations of students from Chubu come now to campus, some of them to occupy scholarships that they graciously named for me, and a handful of Ohio students make their way to Chubu to study Japanese and its culture. I hope this will grow in the years ahead.

When he died a few years ago, the Chubu trustees prepared a handsome bound book in his honor, and I was invited to take one of the speeches that I had given at Chubu and polish it for publication. It was included in the volume honoring Yamada. Much to my surprise, I opened a letter, and there was a check for three thousand dollars as an honorarium, which of course, I returned to the chairman of the board, and said, "I wrote the piece out of affection and regard for a remarkable man, and I want no compensation." It was a small gesture. The next time there was a delegation of Chubu people on campus, knowing my wife's interest in cloisonné, they brought the largest cloisonné vase I've ever seen. It probably would have been less expensive for them if I had accepted the original check,—

SC: [laughs]

CP: but they brought it as a gift, and I simply couldn't refuse. In the larger picture, I think our efforts to build personal relations with universities in Japan, Hong Kong, Southeast Asia, and Southern Africa contributed directly to the growing internationalization of Ohio University.

Presidents Ping and Yamada plant one of 175 flowering cherry trees presented to Ohio University by the Chubu Institute upon OHIO's 175th Anniversary, 1979.

SC: In the mid-1980s sometime, there was a front-page story in the *New York Times* about universities that were being invited by various communities, or by existing educational institutions in Japan, to create campuses there. We were one of those—

CP: [laughs]

SC: mentioned along with Maryland and—

CP: Yes.

SC: I think Johns Hopkins. And I know that you spent a very long time looking into and evaluating whether this would be a prudent move or not. Could you tell us a little about that?

CP: Ah, it's a long tale, and I'll try to keep it short and focused. Komaki City wanted a US university to open a campus, teach US university courses, and offer, at least, a few degree programs. They bought 25 acres of prime land in the area to build a campus for Ohio University, and they had set aside some $25 million for the start of construction. After the conversation had gone on for some time, I made a visit to Komaki City.

    I remember arriving in the Nagoya airport. You would think that I was a celebrity. There were dozens of reporters and television cameras. The mayor of Komaki City greeted me and after some formalities he said, "I want you to go with me to see the site where we will build the Ohio University campus at Komaki." So we got in a helicopter, and we flew and circled the site. Circling our helicopter was a press helicopter that was taking pictures of all this. Anyhow, I met with the city council, and we talked about it, and then I came home.

    We worked seriously with the numbers. We invited the city council to come to Athens, and they came in en masse. We had a dinner at 29 Park Place in their honor. And the Marching 110 came up to serenade the delegation, at my request. Some of the politicians on the city council, who had not traveled much, thought this was the most magnificent thing that they had ever seen and there were tears in their eyes. As we worked with the numbers more and more, I became convinced that while it was a lovely idea, it was, financially, simply not feasible. You could not charge sufficient tuition to make it work. And so I went to the city officials and said, "We are honored, deeply honored, but we simply can't consider it."

SC: I think other institutions did take the plunge and came to discover down the road that you were right, and they had to find some way—

CP: Yes.

SC: to extricate.

CP: Some of them were financial sinkholes that caught universities. But Komaki City stayed very loyal. As my retirement was nearing, I made a courtesy visit to Chubu, and when Komaki officials learned of the visit nothing would do but to have a formal dinner with the city council. One of the things that they were pleased and thankful for was that they had dedicated a new subway line, and for part of this, they created a park.

During their visit, they had been very impressed by the squirrels on the College Green. They wrote and said, "Could you possibly ship us a half-dozen squirrels, hopefully male and female? They would populate the park, and our people would take great delight."

You can't imagine how complicated it is to ship squirrels. Jim Bryant was always willing to build links wherever. He was a great director, vice president for the regional campuses, and international efforts, like the one to Chubu. Jim finally got the squirrels to them, where they turned them loose. I don't know whether they propagated or not, but they were so pleased. So they gave a dinner to honor Claire and me, and the sake flowed freely. I could not take a sip out of my cup without someone refilling it. In Japan, you don't fill your own glass—always someone else—and it can leave you very fuzzy quickly. They presented us with a complete set of china that was made in Komaki City and other nice things.

SC: You talked about a long-standing relationship with Malaysia. Are there other Southeast Asian countries where we were educationally involved?

CP: Definitely. We had a Center for Southeast Asian Studies here on this campus. John Cady was really the founding spirit of that, but a whole host of people contributed to the effort. Let me go back to Malaysia for a minute—

SC: OK.

CP: because it's really quite a story. The beginning goes back to President Sowle's era. The invitation was to teach Ohio University courses and to offer Ohio University degrees: first a BBA and then an MBA. It was a strategic move on the part of the government to get a greater number of Bumiputra, the native Malay people, involved in the business life, banking, and all the commercial enterprises of the country. The Bumiputra were not well represented; business was primarily controlled by minority groups, the Chinese and the Indian population.

Prime Minister Mahathir was very eager to see a higher percentage of Malays involved. And we were asked to work with an institution, which again was a technical institute when we first worked with it. We helped them by offering courses and sending our faculty to spend an extended time there teaching. We had a resident director, Felix Gagliano, serve in that role, and several others—John Schermerhorn, Ellsworth Holden, to mention a few. The resident director and family would spend at least two years in Malaysia as managers in this program. We helped Mara Institute plan and develop a College of Communication and later a College of Engineering. Professor [Robert L.] Savage and others helped them lay it out and develop a curriculum. Over the years, we saw the institute develop until, finally, it began to look like a university.

Mara, in fact, was one of the universities of Malaysia, but it had a distinct mission. That mission was to serve the Malay—the Bumiputra people of the land. As the deputy prime minister said to me when we had

The Malaysian Resource Center at Alden Library: Announcement of Alden as the official depository library of Malaysian materials, 1985. (*Left to right*): Dr. Felix Gagliano, Lian The-Mulliner, President Ping, Professor Tun Abdullah bin Haji Ahmad Badawi (minister of education and later prime minister of Malaysia), Razak Professor Fatimah Hamid Don, and Dr. Hwa-Wei Lee.

him here on campus, "It is our affirmative action effort." It proved to be successful, and after several decades, we essentially worked ourselves out of a job, which was the intent right from the start. We trained faculty, and now they teach the MBA and the BBA. It was in recognition of what that contribution meant to Malaysia that Prime Minister Mahathir accepted the proposal to fund the Tun Abdul Razak Chair. The chair was the first foreign-government-funded chair at a public university in this country.

It has brought to the campus a steady stream of faculty from Malaysia, each in a different discipline. The first one was a very learned Koran scholar and philosopher, and successively they've been in business, education, and a host of disciplines. Their goal is to be intellectual ambassadors and to teach in the Southeast Asia program; secondly, to build the

President Ping with Datuk Dr. Zainal Abidin Abdul Wahid, holder of the Tun Abdul Razak Chair, 1985.

library collection in Alden, which is one of the really strong collections of Southeast Asia material in this country, by identifying material in their discipline, books or whatever, that need to be there to round out the collection. It's been a very successful venture. The idea was that funding from Malaysia for the Razak Chair was to be matched by American corporations doing business in Malaysia.

Spearheaded by Wayne Kurlinski, Ohio vice president for university relations, we ran a major capital campaign in Malaysia. I traveled there, so often that the memories are sort of a blur. We held press conferences periodically where we would announce a sizable gift from this corporation or that corporation; major Malaysian government officials and the American ambassador were always in attendance and very supportive. What the Malaysian contracts brought to campus was a whole core of Ohio faculty who had lived, taught, and done research in Malaysia.

Now our involvement in Thailand was, in part, again with the business school to assist in the development of an institution that was essentially a business college, originally in downtown Bangkok. Bangkok College has become Bangkok University on a magnificent campus now on the out-skirts of Bangkok. We assisted in the development of the curriculum in communications, business, and in other areas, and in the training of faculty. Both have been a very strong relationship, and they have produced loyal pockets of alumni.

We had involvement in Indonesia in much the same way and welcomed to campus a large number of Indonesian students over the years, many of whom have gone back to leadership roles in communication including the managing director of a private television station, and business faculty for the universities in Indonesia. At one time, we had the son of the Indonesian ambassador to the US, as well as the Indonesian consul general. We had the children of all the leading members of the embassy staff, here on campus. When the president of Indonesia was to be entertained at a state visit in Washington, the ambassador included me on the suggested guest list for the White House. So Claire and I were invited. We found our way to the White House and danced side by side with the Reagans, and I rubbed my elbows with some of the political and social elite of both Washington and Indonesia. It was really quite a fun occasion.

SC: Was that your one White House—

CP: That was my one White House visit. We've had several presidents visit the campus over the years. My favorite was Jimmy Carter. We had entertained his mother years before. Miss Lillian came to receive an honorary degree. She was a remarkable woman who late in life had gone to India in the Peace Corps. Much like her son, she was deeply involved in the human condition. When we brought her to campus to give her an honorary degree, the Secret Service asked if she could stay in our home because they felt they could give her more adequate protection there, and she did. A delightful person, as full of life in her eighties as any young person ever was. She stayed several days and got to be close friends with our cook. So one morning, Miss Lillian is in the kitchen having coffee with the cook and jawing. When our daughter, oh I guess Ann Shelton was about sixteen, she was in high school anyway, came down the back stairs as the cook asked Miss Lillian, "How about your love life?"

President Ping holding hands with Lillian Carter, mother of President Jimmy
Carter, while she speaks at the podium, 1979.

SC: [laughs]

CP: [laughs] And Miss Lillian looked up and saw Ann Shelton, and said,
       "Honey, there are some things, perhaps, ought not to be discussed before
       a child your age. Would you excuse us?" [laughs] She was that kind of
       delightful person.

SC: Actually, when her son came to campus, President Carter was expressly
       asked to speak about American education and its internationalization.

CP: Yes. Rich Vedder, distinguished professor of economics, flew down
       to bring him back in the university plane, so he had been well briefed on
       some of the international efforts of Ohio University. President Carter
       acknowledged those efforts and commented on them in the course of his
       speech. He knew that he was at Ohio University and was talking about
       Ohio University.

President Jimmy Carter with OHIO's President Ping in a question and answer session, May 1989.

We gave a dinner in his honor that night. Years had passed since Miss Lillian stayed with us. As President Carter came into our home, Claire and I were standing at the front door greeting our guests. As he came to Claire he leaned over and gave her a kiss on the cheek, and then he said to her, "I just wanted to thank you for being so kind to my mother." Now I don't know that he remembered that or whether someone had briefed him on that but that was such a nice gesture.

President Carter has graced the office of the president, out of office, far more than any other ex-president that I can think of. While on campus, he also agreed to a dialogue with a select group. A faculty group, who was involved in our second ten-year planning effort, Toward the Third Century, and a group of students were selected. We met in Anderson Auditorium in Scripps Hall. Carter didn't speak; he answered questions. And there were some wonderful questions. I remember that I wanted to hug the graduate student who asked a question I thought was so good

—she said, "President Carter, you're known as a religious and moral man." He said, "I am, or try to be." And she said, "You were also the president of the United States." He said, "Yes." Then the student asked, "Was there ever a time when being president created a conflict with your religious and moral convictions?"

Well, this was the kind of question you had to think about. And he said initially, "No, no I don't—yes, there were many times when I wanted to speak out strongly against the violations of human rights by countries that we were allied with from the Philippines to any number of other countries. I was infuriated by what I was told was their handling of human rights." He said, "That need, not to speak because I was president, was a clear conflict."

He thought for another moment and said, "Then there was, for me, an issue of great moment when abortion became an accepted law of the land. I was faced with the reality that as an individual I was adamantly opposed to abortion. But I wasn't just an individual. I was president of the United States, and as president, I was obligated to uphold the law of the land because we are a government, not of men, but of laws."

Then there was a question from a dean—Paul Nelson, the dean of the College of Communication. He and his wife, Judy Pearson, had collaborated on a book. He said to President Carter, "We have something in common. My wife and I have worked on a book, and I know that you and your wife have worked on a book. What are your feelings about co-authoring a book with your wife?" And instantaneously Carter said, "It was the dumbest thing I ever did." He said, "I would sit in the study, and sit before my computer and write, and I was done. Rosalynn would be upstairs in her study, and every word was an agony, and every sentence had to be redone three times, and once written it was not to be changed. I didn't think we ever were going to get done."

Anyhow, it was, I thought, a great visit. In his public address that night in the Templeton-Blackburn Auditorium, he acknowledged Ohio University in so many different ways. You know, many speakers come in for a Kennedy Lecture Series or a special occasion, and they could be anywhere. They don't really take the trouble to find out where they are and to say something about the institution.

SC: We've spent a lot of time talking about the East and visits to South-east Asia. What about Europe? What were our main connections in Europe in your administration?

CP: Well, we send more students to study abroad to Europe than any-where else. We have programs organized by the foreign language faculty in various countries, and I think the key new linkage was the one that was just coming into being at the end of my presidency—the one with Leipzig.

Our efforts in Africa were really most notable because the needs obvi-ously are far greater. Years ago, we had an AID project in Nigeria and an-other one in Kenya, and we still have faculty—like Milt Ploghoft who were involved—and there's a building on the Nigerian campus that is named in Milt's honor. Ted Bernard, and his work in Kenya, has lasted. Anyway, this goes back really to John Baker's and Vern Alden's years. And if you will, let me turn to Africa.

Initially, the College of Education had a leading role. Land grant colleges, like Ohio University, were in the forefront of the AID project efforts. Some in agriculture—we had no role in agriculture—some in health. We had some modest role in health. We had a major role in edu-cation. And, that's what we were doing in Nigeria—helping start a teach-ers college. Later we were invited to help the government of Botswana bring to reality their policy of universal primary education by establish-ing within the University of Botswana a teacher preparation program. We became the educational vehicle for the teaching of teachers. So for fifteen years or longer, we had a core of faculty based in Botswana. We had outstanding leadership in Max Evans. Evans and Luther—

SC: Luther Haseley.

CP: Haseley.

SC: Al Leep, also.

CP: Al Leep and a host of others. Don Knox in Botswana and Swazi-land. Over that period of time, we probably had fifty faculty, from more colleges than I can remember, working in Botswana. We had a handful of people working for years on the project, but one of the clear mandates to the colleges was that it was to be an effort that brought faculty back to Athens, not faculty simply hired to do the tasks in Africa. And it proved to be a wonderful relationship that has blossomed in so many ways.

Botswana is one of the real success stories in southern Africa. It is a functioning democracy that has had changes of leadership by the political process of elections, elections that were transparent. They have a strong educational commitment. And they now have universal primary education and are on the way to developing universal access to secondary education. They have developed a first-rate university, a model for the countries of that region. We have trained some of the faculty for that institution in a variety of disciplines, not just in education. We have a warm and deeply personal relationship. I was invited to participate in the convocation for the proclamation of the independent University of Botswana; it really was my first encounter with the life of the campus, and at that time, it was a small campus—only a few buildings on a dusty plain. The first vice chancellor was actually British. He had been very active in maturing and in nurturing the university, and he became very close to Ohio University and to Claire and me. John Turner.

SC: From the University of Manchester.

CP: Manchester. He was dean of the College of Education at Manchester.

SC: Did we not invite the president of Botswana to receive an honorary degree here? President [Quett Ketumile] Masire—

CP: We did. President Masire was invited to give the commencement address and to receive an honorary degree. I remember vividly. He walked to the podium in the convocation and stood for a moment, and the audience quieted, and he raised his arms and said, "Pula!" Of course, [laughs] that's a little like "Banzai." And he repeated himself, "Pula!" It was pouring rain outside, and he went on to explain to the graduates that they should rejoice in the fact that it was raining on their graduation day. In

Botswana the word for money—the equivalent of a dollar—is "pula," and because it is a dry and arid land "pula" also is the word for rain. Rain is a measure of value. And anyone who is married, or starts a venture, or graduates on a rainy day is blessed. [laughs] He has remained a friend of Ohio University. And the success of the program led to AID inviting us to replicate the effort in Swaziland—

SC: Lesotho, too?

CP: and Lesotho to some degree. Thanks to Don Knox and others, we had some modest success in Swaziland, but nothing like the success in Botswana. During the years that we were active there, I was invited to chair an appointed commission that would advise the university on planning for its future, and how it should it go about it. I spent a month in Swaziland with a team that included the vice chancellor of the University of Zimbabwe, the vice chancellor of the University of Botswana, and a whole series of leading African academics. We held open hearings; we invited community leaders and business people to tell the commission what were their expectations of a university. This was unheard of because they were a British type of a university; they were more British than the British, and they lived in splendid isolation from the needs of the world, and they were a national university, maybe.

We took testimony—I remember the chair of Barclays International was so excited that he had actually interviewed every Swazi person on the Barclays staff; it was the principal bank in the country. He went even in lower management positions to try to identify Swazis who could, in fact, be trained to handle key administrative roles in the effort to really bring Swazis into the business, and let them lead it. He said it was very frustrating and disappointing, because even university graduates were not prepared for the management roles.

We had a plantation owner, who literally had stayed up all night the night before, so he could give his testimony about what sort of training he thought was needed in writing. He wanted to put on paper his thoughts, so he could actually hand the commission something. Anyway it was very fascinating.

Pictured on the steps of the old Baker Center, President Masire of Botswana leaves a luncheon before commencement ceremonies, 1989.

SC: Weren't you involved in something similar for Namibia, trying to help them to—

CP: Well, I have to confess that this Swazi effort didn't go far. The chaos of the government of the land, and the new king and his multiple wives, and all that was going on in the country—

SC: Nothing had changed.

CP: Nothing has changed—in spite of the fact that they had a very strong vice chancellor at the university, a woman scientist.
      The year before I was invited to Namibia, the country had gained its independence. The people had fought guerrilla wars for decades against the occupation of the country by South Africa. The United Nations stepped in to end the conflict and to supervise a national election. It was proclaimed a democracy, and it had independently held its own preelections and chosen the president. The president appointed a commission in 1990 to make recommendations to Parliament on how Namibia should organize its university and teacher training colleges. I was invited to serve on that commission.

SC: Did John Turner—

CP: He was the head of the commission. He and Trevor Coombe were the British presence, and I was the token American presence. As you would suspect, most of the members of the commission were Namibians: a labor leader, a church leader, leaders of the community, and opinion leaders. We spent a month having hearings all over the country where anyone who wanted to could present testimony. We gathered data on the educational scene in Namibia, which was tragically distorted by the apartheid educational system of South Africa. Since Namibia was controlled by South Africa, it meant in essence, you couldn't educate a Namibian beyond the level required for manual labor. You had grammar schools with the teacher/pupil ratio of three hundred to one—and that's absurd—while the small Afrikaans population had an outstanding educational network.

Anyway, we were sworn by the president and granted all sorts of powers to subpoena, and the police were not allowed to interfere or arrest any of us. I never tested the speeding laws of the land, because everybody drove crazily. We spent a month in hearings, in gathering data and documents, and studying the information. And then we went away for an extended period of six or eight months, I've forgotten exactly, and came back for a month to argue our way through a report to Parliament.

Among the recommendations to Parliament was that they abolish the existing university and declare that it had ended. The Afrikaners had such a stranglehold on every important position in the university, and they had tenure. There was no way that you could bring Namibians into university life. There was a highly talented group of Namibians who had been forced to flee the land. Many had been educated overseas and were very able to provide leadership to the university and the country.

We recommended that they establish a new University of Namibia, and a series of teacher training colleges, and a technical college. The technical college would be subcollegiate in its degree-granting authority. We argued at great length, for days, over a whole series of things. I became very close to the group of Namibians serving on the commission.

SC: Peter Katjavivi. I met him at your house.

CP: Peter Katjavivi was the first vice chancellor. Now the president had already chosen him. He met with us in an informal setting in an evening of dinner, dance, and song and not as part of the formal hearings—because he was not yet publicly identified as the person who would be the vice chancellor.

We argued, for example, over the question of tuition. Some of us thought there ought to be fees with a whole system of student financial aid to offset, but that did not fly. Like most African universities, the university was in the then British model that had complete subsidization of student life and the institution. We wrestled, native Namibians were convinced, and they were right that there was a desperate need throughout the country for physicians, and that the new university ought to have a medical school.

I actively opposed the idea, and I argued, "Look at the data, look at the record. You don't have students completing basic science at the elementary and secondary level. You don't have students ready. First, you've got to start with the schooling before they come to the university. Then, maybe, at some future date. Besides, what reason do you have to believe that if you train a physician that he will go out into the hinterland where you see, and rightly see, a desperate need? They're going to stay in the urban areas where the technology, and medicine, and a community of physicians are."

It was one of the most enlightening moments, when I asked the commission, "What reason do you have that they would go to serve this desperate need?" And in a marvelous moment, so descriptive of that moment of the life of Namibia, one of my Namibian colleagues said, "Well, if they're needed, of course they'll go." That was very different than some of the cynical attitudes I saw in other countries.

SC: That was almost twenty years ago. What's happened at the university?

CP: The university has grown, prospered, and has become a presence. But I don't think it has a medical school, however.

SC: And did you go back? Was this when you had your Fulbright, the year after you stepped down as president?

CP: Yes. Well, I actually went back twice. My next assignment was two years after the commission had completed its work. I agreed to chair a commission whose charge was to interview all the Afrikaners remaining on the faculty and to recommend to the governing board which ones should be granted tenure and at what rank. [laughs] So I—

SC: Didn't you know better than to take a pass on that one?

CP: [laughs]

SC: Although it had to be someone from the outside.

CP: Yes. That's right. I chaired the commission, but again we had leading figures in the life of African higher education as members of the commission. We looked at the paper credentials and interviewed—but there was not a day that I went to campus for meetings that I didn't travel with my airline ticket in my one pocket and my passport in the other. It was a very explosive set of recommendations, or it could have been.

Then I went back, you're right. As I left office, I was granted a Fulbright appointment as a senior research scholar. I went back to Namibia and to Botswana and intended to expand it to Zimbabwe, but things got difficult there. Essentially, I was trying, through interviews, to explore what individuals from various sectors wanted from the university. The key question was: What did you expect? I interviewed students, faculty of course, and administrators, but I also—primarily—interviewed the prime minister and key figures in government, key figures in the opposition party, key labor leaders, and business leaders. I was trying to see ways in which there were conflicts and tensions. The university needed to be aware of the expectations and differences among the expectations of several groups. The appointment took me first to Windhoek, Namibia, which got me there in Bob Glidden's first year. I was about as remote from Athens as I could be.

I was out of the way of my successor for a whole year. No one could whisper in my ear. Only one person managed to track me down and that was chairman of the search committee for the University of Nevada at Las Vegas. The search committee was chaired by an English professor that I had had in a higher education management class at Harvard. The committee was interviewing Carol Harter, and he finally found me in Windhoek. I had about an hour-long conversation with him. The conversation that followed was a regular protocol that he apparently asked everybody in his calls, and then he said, "I really have one more question."

I hold Carol Harter in very high regard. She was the president of Geneseo in the SUNY system and decided that she had to leave it—I understand why. She went against my advice to UNLV, and she had a very successful presidency.

Anyway, the final question was, "You know UNLV has had an athletic mess for the last few years. Do you think Carol Harter is tough enough to handle the problem?" And I laughed, and he said, "I think you just answered my question." I said, "That I had." [laughs]

SC: And she was.

CP: And she was.

SC: I think that's a good stopping point.

CONVERSATION
with
SAM CROWL

May 24, 2011

SC: Charlie, one of the concerns when you arrived on campus, and these are always concerns in tight budget times, was the faculty felt that its voice was not being heard. And the way in which the administration was structured meant that the academic vice president was just one of many whose voice competed with many others for funding.

One of the things that you did, that we have talked about, was to come in with a new model of the president and the provost. The provost shared the Office of the President and both were academic officers, so academics were placed right at the center of the administrative structure.

And then you went to work to involve faculty in the decision-making process of the University. I know that I was surprised when the University Planning Advisory Committee, the Budget Advisory Committee really, was put together, and all members of the Faculty Executive Committee became standing members of that committee. Could you talk a little bit about what you were trying to accomplish in making the faculty play a significant role in the governance of the University?

CP: Let me add a footnote to the description of the administrative structure. One of the reasons for doing it this was way, or describing it this way, was that, as president, I wanted to be very active with the academic life of the campus and deeply involved in academic issues. I didn't want to be walking on the toes of an academic vice president, so the provost and I shared the office in a variety of ways including the presidential involvement in academic matters. It was clear to me that one of the seething issues on campus was conflict between the administration and faculty. That's never going to go away completely. There's just something about the roles that dictate it. But because I regarded myself as a faculty member, I tried consciously to build strong bridges. And the Faculty Senate was an obvious place to start. I also tried to work with the Distinguished Professors, the University Professors, and a whole series of different groups.

With the Faculty Senate, I made it a practice of having lunch with them monthly, and letting them sound off or talk about anything that they wanted to talk about. When we put together a campus-wide planning committee, I used the faculty's chosen leadership of the Senate as a determining factor, and I brought the whole, as you pointed out, executive committee onto this university-wide planning committee. I also tried to make it regularly a part of my routine to go to the Faculty Senate meetings, monthly meetings, and stand, much like the parliamentary model, for questions. I am a philosopher by training, and I frankly enjoy that kind of give and take. Sometimes it was mostly take, but I was quite willing to give, and I did try to listen.

I think that Neil Bucklew and Jim Bruning were very helpful in being an integral part of that effort. They were, I think, genuinely accepted by the faculty as academic leaders. I think gradually as we went through a series of chairs of the Faculty Senate, beginning with Dick Bald and moving through—you were a chair somewhere in there, I've forgotten—

SC: After Dick Bald.

CP: a whole series of really fine people.

SC: Roger Rollins, Duane Schneider, Ted Bernard, Patti Richard—

CP: I remember Patti Richard particularly. We have been close friends ever since her service on the executive committee. After one luncheon meeting

Pictured in a classroom in 1981, Professor Patricia "Patti" Richard stands in front of a chalkboard that says, "In Vitro Veritas." Richard was chair of the Faculty Senate and a member of the University Planning Advisory Committee (UPAC).

broke up, we were walking down the hall, and I was walking with Patti. She said, "You know, you're really not as bad as I thought you were."

SC: [laughs]

CP: [laughs] Which was a high compliment because she had a [laughs] . . . mind-set prone to be antiadministration or suspicious of the administration.

SC: Skeptical.

CP: "Skeptical," good word. They began to see that decisions being debated in the University Planning Advisory Committee (UPAC) or decisions coming out of that committee were, maybe, not the decisions the faculty wanted, but decisions in which they clearly had a voice. And, decisions that were not just empty exercises in planning. They translated into the budget.

SC: Yes, and when I think of the original sixteen members of the UPAC, which may have gotten a little larger as it went on, eight of them were faculty members.

CP: Yes.

SC: At what point did you see that this system, or process, was working in the way in which you hoped it would work? Was there a eureka moment?

CP: No, there was no eureka moment. It just seemed to gradually build, and the resistance and antagonism began to erode over time. There are some members of the Faculty Senate who are always going to be antagonistic with the president. At my last Faculty Senate meeting, as I was getting ready to turn over the keys to Bob Glidden, and to go happily on my way, I said to the Faculty Senate that I had kept track of the number of questions I had been asked. One of the intriguing parts of that analysis was that a high percentage of the questions had been asked by one of the senators.

I said, "If only once, he had been asking me a question where he wanted an answer instead of making a statement"—this was frequently the case when asking questions on the floor of the Senate—"I would have been delighted to try to answer it." But he never did.

I was pleased and touched that I was presented with a citation in which they suggested that all the kind things being said about me were probably serving me ill because my head was swelling. They said they were honored by the fact that I had been responsive. They named me Senator for life, and the citation was signed by all the Faculty Senate chairs I had served with. [laughs]

SC: That was punishment. [laughs]

CP: [laughs] Yes, being honored by attending all Senate meetings sounds a little bit like Sartre's hell. [laughs] Anyhow, I think, in the end, it was a working relation. Not always in harmony but a good working relation.

SC: In most academic worlds and most academic systems, the entrepreneur professors learn to circumvent the system and run around it, and take their ideas right to the president if they want—

CP: Yes.

SC: a study in Rome program, or want a new lab to do something that hasn't been done before. And your system was built on the president denying those requests and saying that the route was through a grant-making—

CP: Yes.

SC: process, where you convinced the planning unit you were a part of, or the department you were a part of, to sponsor such an idea and put in a request for seed money. Did those two ever come in conflict, or did you ever have to say "No" to a faculty member that you later regretted? Were there times—particularly I'm thinking now of Tom Wagner and John Gaddis—where you found ways to be supportive even if it wasn't directly through the UPAC process?

CP: Well, this was a very deliberate decision. If there were two routes to decision making, one directly through the president and one through the whole structure of the UPAC, you really had a problem. And, I think I consistently avoided that. I'm trying to think of the times that I stepped outside of it.

    One time I did was with Dick McFarland, who was an electrical engineering professor—very active in contributing to our success in avionics—and he came to me and said, "I want to complain and make a suggestion. I think the way we have structured our grant pattern is inhibiting the development of additional research proposals. If we could find some way to return a portion of the overhead to the unit that was, in fact, initiating

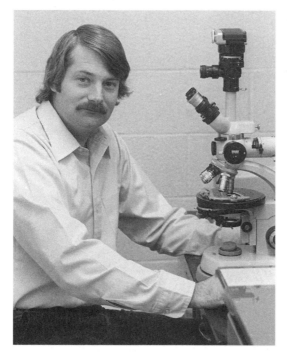

Thomas E. Wagner, University faculty leader and breakthrough researcher (named Distinguished Professor of Molecular and Cellular Biology in 1993), seated at his microscope, 1980.

the successful proposal for outside funding, I think that would be great seed money, and I think it would be the smart thing for the University to do." At the time UPAC didn't exist. It just seemed to me, after the conversation with Neil, such a good idea that that's what we did. And it has paid off handsomely.

Tom Wagner came, and he was always a favorite because he was an exciting researcher doing breakthrough work. I said, "Tom, I fully support what you are trying to do, but I think you have to go through the UPAC process, or alternatively, make an 1804 proposal." Which he did. It was rated highly as it moved through the review. The whole idea of pushing things through UPAC was to let others establish the relative importance of a particular idea and to think about it. I didn't always agree with it and would sometimes act contrary to it, but I always felt that I had to explain myself to UPAC when I did.

I don't remember that I did it with John Gaddis. I think that I encouraged him. I certainly was supportive of the proposals that he submitted.

(*Left to right:*) President Ping, Yale University historian Paul M. Kennedy, and Distinguished Professor of History John L. Gaddis, commencement 1989.

And I, with John's and your help, worked with John Baker to establish the Baker Peace Studies Program on campus. It was housed in the Contemporary History Institute. I think that the institute itself is one of the jewels in our crown.

SC: When you arrived on campus you circulated to maybe 10 or 15 or 20 faculty members who must have been identified as campus leaders, saying that you planned to make two speeches in your first year, and you wanted some help and guidance from them in identifying issues that should go in one or the other. One, you planned to make a broad or more general statement about higher education, at that moment, and the life of the University and the nation. And the other, perhaps addressing more specific local issues, but as it turned out, you gave the more specific issues talk first.

In it, I remember that you identified a number of faculty members who impressed you and the sort of work that they were doing. Once again, was this conscious? What was behind the effort, during a very troubled time, to decide that the first group that you were going to speak to was the faculty doing the sorts of things they normally do—teaching and research?

CP: I believe in, and continue to believe that it is the faculty, broadly defined, who do the productive work of the institution. The administration is here to help make that possible. I wanted to understand what was going on: What was promising in the thinking of the faculty? What were they troubled about? Among other things, I hosted a series of teas, sherry and tea, at our home in the late afternoon. We invited all the Distinguished Professors, in small groups of two or three, and all the University Professors, and a handful of others. I began to get to know people and to hear from them. I hoped I was a good listener; I tried to be.

SC: In all my dealings with you, both as a faculty member and for eleven years as an administrator, I don't ever remember you misremembering something. I never remember having a conversation in which we came to an agreement, and then lo and behold a month later, I would have to remind you of what we had said. What was the technique that you used to keep track, because I wouldn't get, at least from you in these more casual meetings, some memo of understanding afterwards. Did you write one every time we had a meeting?

CP: I don't know that I wrote one every time, but any time there was an important issue, I would write a memo to file, just to jog my own memory. And frequently, I'd write a letter to the person with whom I had talked and describe my sense of where our conversation ended—a sort of Quaker style of leading. I would write, "If your sense is different, please let me know."

SC: Well, it was certainly true that one of the hallmarks of the daily work with you and with Neil and with Jim was that all three of you had the ability to remember and to have a good recall of conversations. Now most of the things that I probably was discussing with all three of you were not of a magnitude where we had to be very certain of what it was that we agreed to, but I was just impressed with that.

CP: Well, you know, there were some of them that were very important. I remember one vividly. After we began to put in place a whole series of tests to try to measure what we were doing, one of the tests, which I sarcastically referred to as a "happiness quotient," measured student reaction as freshmen and as seniors. We learned a lot of things because we could disaggregate the data. We learned about problems that particular colleges had. We could provide some evidence of problems.

    Student retention was a key element in our enrollment management, and in fact, *the* key element because the purpose of any college is, in fact, to lead a student to a degree. That means they're here over time. And, our retention pattern was very bad, which was one of our sources of the enrollment problems. We had a revolving door and—

SC: And one of the things studying the issue revealed was—contrary, I think, to faculty assumption—that the revolving door had lots of "B" students in it—

CP: Yes.

SC: not just "D" students.

CP: Yes. There wasn't any question that we were accepting students who had a questionable background for college work in 1975, and through the rest of the '70s, because we were eager for enrollment. When we put these broad survey-type questionnaires in place, one of the things that just jumped out from the data was that the student who came on campus without a declared major, or without interest sufficient to declare a major as a freshman, felt poorly served by their academic advising.

    You and I talked about this, and you came up with the idea of enlisting a core of faculty who would agree to be the advisors of the uncommitted students. They agreed, I mean those who had volunteered, to do some training sessions. When we annually looked at the data, that group of students changed in their perception.

SC: And once again, relying on faculty as sort of mentors to the intellectual life, so that students at least were given the opportunity to become more comfortable with talking with a faculty member outside of the classroom, in an office conversation, about what they were thinking about.

CP: Sam, I don't know whether I stole it from you, or you stole it from me, but that's one of the ways I described the role of faculty in academe, mentors to the intellectual life.

SC: I stole it from you. [laughs]

CP: I have no pride of ownership. [laughs]

SC: Yes, it was, once again, the breakdown of the faculty-student relationship, advisor to advisee. It was something that was a product of the late '60s, and I know when the students listed their demands on a big blackboard in Mem Aud in '68 or '69, one of the things was, "No more faculty advisors signing off." Students used to have their faculty advisor sign off on their registration form. The faculty was very happy to give that up. They said, "Fine. You can have that one." We realized a decade later that that had been a mistake, and it was not a healthy academic policy.

That makes a nice segue into students. The first thing that you did was to hire a new director of admissions.

CP: Yes.

SC: Jim Walters—

CP: Yes.

SC: who turned out to be a wonderful director of admissions. One of the things that he began to chip away at, I think, almost from the time that he got here, even though we were having difficulty in retaining students and maybe even attracting some, was contemplating the move to selective admissions. Can you describe the process of the decision making that led to that move? I think it was the late '70s.

CP: It was actually later than that.

SC: Was it?

CP: Yes. Jim Walters brought together a team of admissions counselors, a really able group, and they worked well. We looked at this again and at the surveys. One of things you learned from this very quickly is that a visit to campus is an important element in the decision to come to Ohio University. Therefore, the smart thing to do was to figure out ways to get people to visit the campus, which we did. Jim Walters organized students to direct and to lead tours. A whole series of things in the first planning document was the product of the initial phase in working with and establishing the planning process and to focus that planning around institutional values. We identified six basic commitments, and they became sort of touchstones. [laughs] With some mild optimism and that document, we also addressed the problem of enrollment. We said in that planning document that we would grow in numbers only insofar as that growth was consistent with growth in quality. Now, like many such pronouncements that was an aspiration rather than a fact.

I think that we were really open door admissions because of the enrollment problem, and the drain that it brought to our budget. But if you retain students, and you get students to their junior and senior year, that has a handsome financial dividend, given how the state calculates the state subsidy.

When the number of applications we had was far larger than the proposed size of the freshman class, we began to move toward the possibilities of selective admission. We finally implemented selective admission

A Green Carpet Day tour group on the historic Ohio University College Green with Cutler Hall and McGuffey Hall in the background, 1981.

in about 1983. We were moving towards it. Then ten years later, when we went to summarize a similar extended planning cycle, and we came out with a new ten-year planning document, the theme was: We were a college, a university, of a particular type. We were by commitment a residential university, and we were determined that we would grow in size only so long as numbers are consistent with the community. This was the second pronouncement ten years later—

SC: Right.

CP: only insofar as that growth was consistent with the nature of the institution. I don't know what that point is, but I think there is a point where institutions simply change their character by the number of students enrolled.

SC: True. Beyond that number we tried to limit growth. The selective admissions process differed from college to college. In some cases, as in engineering, it was required that you had to have achieved a certain level in calculus, physics, and chemistry in high school, because beforehand, students were entering engineering who had not, and they were doomed, obviously, to failure. And in business and communication, which had become increasingly popular majors, the University made a decision that we wanted to keep a balance between the professional colleges. We didn't want any one or two to get way out ahead of the others in term of enroll-ment growth.

CP: Yes.

SC: So the rule of thumb I recall—I don't believe it appeared in any planning document—was that we wanted to hold all of the professional colleges to about 20 percent of the enrollment growth. So—of just the freshman enrollment—that allowed us to institute selective admissions, selectively. [laughs]

CP: A student applying, applied directly to a college for admission.

SC: Right.

CP: And some were admitted to the University,

SC: That's correct.

CP: but not to the college.

SC: But that's also how we managed, with a steady freshman class of about 3,000 over about fifteen years to increase enrollment because we kept—

CP: The students were still with us—

SC: Exactly.

CP: into senior year.

SC: I think our retention rate, as I recall, went from something like 67 percent to a high of about 84 percent or 85 percent, or maybe even higher than that.

CP: Higher than that. Yes, and that's comparable with the best of the public universities and even some of the very good private universities.

SC: On a commitment level, I think when I got here half of the freshman class had been in the top half of their high school class. By the time I stepped down as the dean of University College in 1992, or roughly at the end of your presidency, something like 80 percent had been in the top 20 percent.

CP: Yes.

SC: When we began, we began to make progress on both ends. That was important.

CP: Yes, and in fairness, part of the scene was the times. You know, in the '70s, we still had the lingering impact of the Vietnam War, the draft, and the basic proposition that the student faced was a choice between hanging around the streets and being drafted or going to college, which seems like a better option. If you had a choice between going into the military or going to college, which seems the better option? Speaking of the military, this reminds me of something that I think is part of this history and that probably ought to be recorded.

My first year here, in 1975, we received an official communication from the Department of the Army saying that they were withdrawing our Army ROTC unit for lack of successful degree completion, the lack of officer production. Well, we were hungry for students, and ROTC students, at least some, were supported in their education. Jim Abraham, who was at the time the adjutant general responsible for the State Guard [Ohio National Guard], was also having a problem with State Guard recruitment. He and I, in conversation, began to put an idea together. We went to the Pentagon to talk with them about this idea. The idea was that a scholarship would be granted to a student enlisting in the Ohio National Guard, and that student would be a part of the ROTC unit on campus. It was a way of addressing both problems.

We made our way into the Pentagon, and we earnestly sold it to a couple of senior officers. The proposal was eventually adopted as an experiment here. It proved famously successful, and it was used as a model across the nation. Today we have a very strong ROTC program, a program that year after year wins first place awards for everything from academic achievement to physical conditioning, and a strong State Guard. I'm very proud of that fact, and Jim Abraham, who is in his nineties, is also very proud of that fact. I have been inducted into the ROTC Hall of Fame and honored at a dinner by the State Guard group. I think ROTC has been a healthy presence, and I defended it. That was a time when faculties were basically skeptical of ROTC programs—

SC: And students.

CP: I steadfastly insisted that ROTC is a safeguard. If we had our military officers trained only in a military academy, without the leavening influence of a university campus, I think it would be a tragic condition. I rejoice in the fact that people like General [Robert] Arter, who went on to be a three-star general, came through our ROTC program. The leadership of the army is not all at West Point. When you are on the West Point or Annapolis campus, there is a different quality to life. Everything is pretty ruled, you know. The academies have fine faculties, and I'm sure in class there is great freedom, but it's a different kind of exposure to higher education.

SC: A different campus culture, too.

CP: Yes, indeed.

SC: Charlie, I remember being struck at one commencement when a student leader stood up as part of the program, and before she talked about whatever her specific role was in the ceremony she wanted to tell a personal story. She was an African American student from St. Louis, and the story that she told, I recall, was that she came here a long, long way from home. Her mother was worried about her, as mothers are, and when her mother came to the Parents Weekend reception in her fall quarter, here at your house, she said, "You know, I worry about my daughter, and I want you to take good care of her." The result of that conversation was that every quarter that this student was on campus you wrote her mother a letter giving her an update on how she was doing. Now, tell me how often you did something like that, and what other devices did you come up with to establish a personal relationship with at least some students, when that's probably the most difficult thing for a president to do?

CP: My, Sam, that goes back a lot of years. The student's name was Donna Jones, and she's from St. Louis, but it wasn't at the parents' reception, it was at Precollege.

SC: OK. So it started right away.

CP: Her mother came up to me and shook her finger in my face and said, "You take good care of my little girl." Donna's not a small woman, and I said, "We'll try." Donna and I became good friends and still stay in touch, and I think she is currently on the alumni board. It was a wonderful relationship.

SC: And did you, in fact, write her mother two or three times a year?

CP: Yes, I don't think I wrote every quarter. I did write from time to time.

SC: And were there any other students that you counseled?

CP: Yes. I can't remember all of them, but I remember once receiving a call from a frantic student who said, "My mother's ill. I need help. What can I do?" And I went down and tried to help. We got an ambulance there to take care of her. I tried to meet and respond to students, not just through the established structures of the Student Senate and student organizations.

Claire and I had a seemingly endless round of dinners at fraternity and sorority houses. And I tried to certainly meet with students who were recognized leaders. But also to shortcut that process. Occasionally, I would go down and eat in the dining halls. Then when they came to me to complain the food was terrible, I said, "I was just down there last week, and I thought it was pretty good." [laughs]

I had regular open meetings in residence halls. Not long after I started, I quietly began to teach a course every year in the philosophy department and occasionally in the Higher Education Program. Mostly, frankly, to relieve my endless cycle of reading all the stuff that sat on my desk and instead having to read Kierkegaard and Hegel and—

SC: As a break. [laughs]

CP: As a relief! [laughs]

SC: We were talking, before we started to record this session, about some memories of some basketball players, and you told a wonderful story that I wish you would repeat because, I think, it will amuse some people who followed the basketball team closely in the Danny Nee era. It has to do with Dave Jamerson, who was a very fine three-point shooter on the Nee clubs, and the first year of Larry Hunter. Dave had blown out a knee, and you would run into him while working out at the Convocation Center. Go ahead and tell the story.

CP: First of all, Dave Jamerson wasn't just a fine three-point shooter, he was a superb three-point shooter. We had guests from Malaysia and had a formal dinner at the house, and I said, "Would you like to go to a basketball game?" And they said, "We'd be delighted." So I took them to the basketball game. They had never seen a basketball game. And that was the night that Dave Jamerson set an NCAA record. I don't remember what the record was, but it was an extraordinary performance. He only missed two shots from a three-point range the whole night, and one of them was because he got knocked on his ass by the defensive player. [laughs]

SC: I think he made fourteen three-point shots that night and scored sixty points.

CP: It just was a beautiful performance. He is such a fine young man. Oh, the finish of the Malaysians story—we were taking them back to their guest quarters, and I said, "Did you enjoy the game?" There was a pause, and our guests said, "Yes, yes. It was fun, but I didn't see much to it. You throw the ball up, and it goes through the hoop." [laughs]

SC: [laughs]

CP: Anyhow, Dave did serious damage to his knee. I, of course, going back even to my high school days, have had a series of knee problems and knee operations. They've whittled on my knees so many times that I was tempted to suggest that they just put in zippers, rather than sutures. It would be easier for all of us. Anyway, Dave and I, at least, became acquainted in the training room at the Convo, and I happened to overhear a conversation as Dave was rehabbing his knee.

Dave began to be able to shoot and to practice; he was a dedicated perfector of his skill. On that same team was another basketball player named [Paul] "Snoopy" Graham, who was probably as good a natural athlete as I've ever seen. He could do things that you couldn't believe possible while he was leaping to the basket and changing the shot he originally intended to make. Snoopy happened to be out practicing, for a change, with Dave. Snoopy turned to Dave and said, "I wish I could shoot like you." I was close enough to overhear this conversation. Dave turned to him and said, "Snoopy, you start a million shots behind."

SC: [laughs]

CP: [laughs] He was probably right. Dave didn't have the natural talent, but he had the discipline. Both of them went on to brief careers, at least, in the National Basketball Association. Dave Jameson became a full-time worker with the Ohio Campus Crusade. Snoopy, I've lost touch with.

But I had from that same era an e-mail from one of the players, who I confess when I saw the name I didn't recognize, whose son had graduated that year from Findlay College. He said he remembered my coming into the locker room, as I tried to do after many games, sometimes to console them and sometimes to applaud their performance. His son was in the Findlay College graduating class, and he had received the statewide award that is given every year in my name by the Ohio Campus Compact for outstanding community service. He said when he heard that his son was presented with the Charles J. Ping Award that it just brought back a flood of good memories. I was pleased that he took the initiative.

Let me tell one other story. I love football. I played and coached at both the high school and collegiate level. The head coach when I came had been here for years, and he was a very beloved coach—

SC: Bill Hess.

CP: Bill Hess. I made it a point to go into the locker room after every home game, again to say something to them. We played Cincinnati here, and we were leading with just minutes to go and had the ball within inches of a first down. Bill Hess made the decision to go for the first down, rather than punting the ball. Of course, they didn't make it, and Cincinnati took the ball, and after a couple of passes, they were within field goal range. They kicked a field goal and won by one or two points. I went into the locker room, and it was absolutely silent. And there was Bill Hess sitting on a stool mumbling to himself saying, "Stupid, stupid, stupid." I came up behind him, not intending to startle him, and I said, "You're right, Coach." And he turned around, and he had his fist cocked, and he was ready . . .

OHIO head football coach Bill Hess (1958–77), ca. 1970s. After President Ping arrived on campus, he and Bill Hess forged a good relationship.

SC: [laughs]

CP: [laughs] Bill Hess, sadly, later developed cancer and died a lingering death. He was a wonderful person.

SC: Let's move from one universe to quite another. We've been talking about events and people internal to the campus, and that's what those of us on campus know about. But a president has another life, a life dealing with external constituencies that most of us on campus have no idea about.

CP: Yes.

SC: What are those experiences? Let's start with the state of Ohio, and share whatever memories you have, or stories you'd like to tell, about your interaction with the governors. You would have served when Jim Rhodes was governor, and when Dick Celeste was governor, and when our own George Voinovich was governor. Then we'll move to talk about some legislative leaders who were important, and then talk a little bit about the board of regents. What are your memories and impressions of the governors you had to deal with?

CP: Well, Governor Rhodes was very uncomfortable on campus, and he was always in a hurry to get off campus whenever he came.

SC: Kent State probably had—

CP: Yes, I'm sure.

SC: something to do with that.

CP: He was scarred by Kent State, as we all were. He was a difficult man to deal with, and unlike governors I had worked with in Michigan, he rarely consulted university presidents about important issues like the appointment of trustees. He'd just snatch a name out of the air that somebody had suggested to him. So I had very little influence with him in terms of trustee appointments.

   But I did have some trustees who had some real influence with him. I remember going with Kenner Bush, the third generation of his family to serve as a trustee and the editor and publisher of the *Athens Messenger,* and a good Republican and a great trustee; and Dean Jeffers, who was the CEO of Nationwide Insurance. We went because we needed a new Aquatic Center. Nationwide had expressed an interest in this project and ended up giving us a grant of $350,000 to have an architectural competition, which is the way you ought to build buildings. The Capital bill had been released in a draft form of recommendations from the regents.

   Let me back up. The operating budget for institutions is largely a product of a formula-driven model of funding that you can influence only

(*From left*): Acting Dean Gerald A. Faverman, President Ping, and Governor James Rhodes at the dedication of the new Youngstown regional facility for the College of Osteopathic Medicine.

at the margin. The Capital bill is highly politicized, and to our disappoint-ment, the new Aquatic Center to replace the old Natatorium was not in the budget. That meant you had to figure out somehow to get it added to the bill when it comes from the governor's office as a recommendation.

So Kenner and Dean went with me to meet with Governor Rhodes. It was a fairly typical session with Governor Rhodes. We three guests were there to plead our case and all the time that we were there he was talking to at least three assistants doing one thing or another, and he was taking phone calls on two phones. As we got up to leave—Governor Rhodes' attention span was not long—Kenner said to Dean, "I'm not sure he heard us at all." Apparently, Rhodes heard the comment because as we were going toward the door he looked up, and he said, "Dean, I'll not for-get your old swimmin' hole." And it showed up in the Capital bill. [laughs]

SC: [laughs]

CP: I think the next of my cherished memories was about the buildings for regional clinical sites of the College of Osteopathic Medicine. One of the things that came with it is a series of regional teaching centers, which was part of our model. We'd teach the clinical program at local hospitals; we had four sites around the state, one of which had been determined more by the politics within the legislature. A new handsome building had been built in Youngstown. Anyway, a very influential senator from that area, Senator [Harry] Meshel, was a Democrat from Youngstown, but there was good collaboration between Rhodes and Democrats. The governor invited me to fly over with him to dedicate a new building at our regional site. I had just recently come back from one of my early visits to China. I had returned visits to several campuses, and listened to the endless stories of faculty, administrators, and intellectuals who had been sent off to work in the coal mines or rice paddies as a way of—

SC: Reeducation.

CP: Yes, during the Cultural Revolution. They had lost a whole section of their life. And this concept of intellectuals being sent off to work for some reason came up in the course of my conversations with Governor Rhodes, who had no great love for faculty, I think.

SC: He thought it was a great idea, probably. [laughs]

CP: I saw the wheels turning in his head, "What a good idea!" [laughs]

SC: [laughs] Mao and Rhodes.

CP: Governor Celeste was my favorite, and we began working together, talking anyway, while he was still a candidate. I shared with him an idea that had been fermenting in a national movement, a program of excellence, and some of the parts that I thought ought to be included in comprehensive programming. Governor Celeste was one of those wonderful people in politics who listened closely to an idea, and, if he thought it was a good idea, he would run with it, and it became his.

The Excellence Program that Governor Celeste instituted and saw that it was funded during his two terms, was, I think, the most comprehensive Excellence Program of any state. It really did reach out to campuses. It was not just a way to build the quality of academic life, but simply it was designed to use campuses to find some way to address the problems of the rust belt. That is, to get ideas that had economic potential rolling in Ohio with a larger focus on quality of campus programs.

There was a whole series of things: There was a statewide undergraduate program competition; and there was an Excellence Professorship that had to be matched by a $500 matching gift. There were—

SC: $500,000.

CP: Yes, $500,000. And, there was a particular focus on programs that had economic consequences. Anyhow, it was a broad, comprehensive effort that, I think, had very positive outcomes.

SC: Certainly for us it did.

CP: Yes. It certainly did here. We were very successful in the competition to get a number of Excellence Awards. I thought the program was a measure of the remarkable stature of the man. Governor Celeste was a Rhodes Scholar; he was an intellectual of the first rate. After his two terms as governor he left office. He was next involved in politics in Washington. Then he went on to a college presidency in Colorado Springs as the president at Colorado College.

SC: Yes, he was remarkable as a governor, as I recall, coming with his wife and spending nights on college, in dormitories.

CP: Well, his wife was an interesting woman. I don't think she came with him. She was her own person. As she said to Claire on several occasions, "I am not going to let the fact that my husband happens to be governor interfere with my life." And it didn't as far as I could tell. I think, when

Dick came, it was wonderful for both universities and for him. He made the rounds of all the universities.

SC: Right.

CP: He generally only taught one class, or occasionally more than one, and he stayed in the residence halls. When he came here, we had planned a reception at the end of his visit. He was to be delivered to my office, so I could escort him to the reception.

He came to Cutler Hall, and he said, "Charlie, is it all right if I close the door because I want to talk to you for a minute?" I said, "Sure." We sat down, and he said, "I have one basic question." I said, "All right." He said, "How do you manage to dupe all these students? Here you are, there are not one hundred universities your size or larger, and all

President Ping accepting an award for undergraduate education on behalf of Ohio University from Governor Richard Celeste.

these kids think that they're on a small college campus. Now there's something different about the life here. How do you do it?" I laughed, and I said, "I don't know. But I'm pleased to have that shared with me," and we talked for some time about factors that contributed to it. I think the faculty-student interaction is the key. Then we went on to the reception.

SC: You also did at least once, maybe more, take foreign trips with Celeste—

CP: Yes.

SC: as part of the state economic development? In fact, maybe traveled to China?

CP: Yes. Well, it was by invitation of the governor. Basically, the party that was put together was businesspeople, and Governor Celeste asked me to travel with them. I'm not quite sure why, but I think university presidents, at the time, were certainly considered decorative in China. I enjoyed it because I got to know a whole group of businesspeople, and I got to know well both Dick Celeste and his wife.

   Those long, long plane rides. I remember on one of the trips when we flew directly from Columbus to Shanghai. We changed planes in Seattle and in Tokyo, and then we arrived in Shanghai. The governor's aide came back to where I was seated and said, "Charlie, the plane's a little late, and we have a dinner engagement in Shanghai, which is going to be optional for all the businesspeople in the party, but it's not optional for you. You go." I said, "Okay."

SC: [laughs]

CP: You know after that kind of a trip, you're sort of bleary eyed and vague. So I went into the lavatory and tried to shave and clean up as best I could and pulled a clean shirt out of my carry-on luggage and went to dinner.

   Our host was the parent of a prominent architect in Cleveland. The family had been a very prosperous family in Shanghai, and the house, a palatial home in its heyday, must have been an absolutely spectacular sight. The Communist government had decided that this was too much space for one family, so ten families had been allotted space to live in this house. It had been misused and abused, but now the new regime had returned it back to the family. They had this slightly used building, more than slightly used, this painfully used building as their home. The dinner was held there.

I was seated next to the wife of our host. It was a lovely evening, but one of the customs of China in such formal banquets is, starting with the host, there is a toast and you "Ganbei," which means to drain. So you're drinking this white lightning that they call brandy. After a while, it's sort of a chin in the soup, and I remember getting a little fuzzy towards the end of the banquet. Our host got up to speak, I remember the picture to this day.

If you were to send a request to central casting and ask, "Send me someone who looks like a Confucian figure," this is the man that would be sent from central casting—a stringy little beard, a slender little man, and a quiet nice person. Speaking through the official translator, that is, the Communist government–appointed translator, he extended his greetings to the governor and his party. He said how honored he was that on our first night in China we would come to his home and have dinner, and he went on in that vein. As he finished the speech, he picked up his glass and there was a pause as he obviously prepared his final line, and he said, "And I am a capitalist! Ganbei!" [laughs]

SC: [laughs]

CP: We all drank to that, and there was a kind of awkward pause while the translator figured how to translate it. Finally, he translated it honestly.

Anyway, I enjoyed working with Governor Celeste both at the personal and at the official level. He was very responsive to campuses. He consulted with the presidents about trustees, identifying the people that he was considering. He would listen to your proposals, and much to my joy, he gave me two or three ardent Republicans. I think Jenny Grasselli Brown, Ralph Schey, the CEO of a major company in Cleveland and a wonderful trustee, as was Jenny.

SC: A rarity that a—

CP: that a Republican governor would appoint someone active with the other party—

SC: Or a Democrat.

CP: Yes, or a Democratic governor would appoint an active Republican. I was riding with Celeste in the governor's limousine, and he turned to me and said, "I've given you the last two. The next one is mine." I smiled and said, "I'm sure that the person will be a good trustee." Not just good but great: Charlotte Eufinger.

I remember being invited to—well, I had been in the governor's mansion for a number of events—for a dinner where we were hosting a CEO of Honda, which was one of the offshoots of these trips. The Honda Company had been instrumental, not only in investing billions of dollars in a production plant in Ohio,—

SC: In Marysville.

CP: They saw that their suppliers relocated in strategic places. One of which was a Tokyo seat company that opened for business with a factory here in Athens, and, unfortunately, chose some years later to move closer to Marysville. But it was here as a major employer for a time. I was seated next to the president of Honda, and in the course of the dinner, I thanked him for the Tokyo seat plant and its impact on the Athens economy. I went on to say how delighted we were to have a plant in Athens, Ohio, because there was so little growth in employment opportunities and so little manufacturing in the area.

He took all this in, and he smiled and said, "Yes, it was a carefully made decision." He said, "We toured three or four possible locations before we came to Athens, not alerting anyone to the fact that we were coming. We came on a very hot summer day. As we drove around the campus, we were so pleased to see a number of Japanese students walking the campus."

Ohio had a long-standing link to Chubu University. Every summer, they would send groups to campus for a period of intensive English. To our good fortune, the president of Honda happened to tour the area when these Japanese students were on campus. Then he paid the nicest compliment to Athens. He said, "Athens is the Kyoto of Ohio." And, if you have ever been to Kyoto—

SC: Yes. [laughs]

CP: it is indeed the ancient capital, a lovely, lovely place. It's the only place I've ever visited where your anticipation of visiting, from *National Geographic*, or wherever you've seen pictures, was exceeded by the actual, visual experience.

SC: Good story.

CP: I think it turned out that we ended up offering some English language courses to the Japanese executives who came to Marysville, at least—

SC: so that was a symbiotic relationship—

CP: of language and culture.

SC: Right, right.

CP: And, yes it was.

SC: Now, the Voinovich years, at least at the beginning, were a little tougher economically. There had been a pinch at the end of the late '80s, after the Reagan years. I guess we'd call it the Bush recession or whatever, so that there was a contraction, I remember, in the budget, and we were back into budget cutting rather than a gradual growth. What was your relationship with Voinovich and was it ever hampered because he had gone to school here? I mean, the sense being that he couldn't be seen as bending over backwards to throw us any favors.

CP: Oh, no. We had been personal friends for many years. When he was mayor of Cleveland, I admired the extraordinary job that he did in turning around that desperate situation, and I quickly became friends with him. When he became governor, he was open to the fact that he was an Ohio University graduate, and he was quick to honor that relationship. He had great admiration for John C. Baker, who had been instrumental in his career here in helping him to decide, as a student politician, which direction he would go.

He was helpful, but there was clearly no love lost between Governor Voinovich and Governor Celeste. His coming into office meant that most of the programs in higher education that Celeste had authored and had a close identification with him withered and died.

Voinovich continued the concern of the Edison Centers and the economic development potential of using campuses. He was very good about that, and we were richly rewarded for our early involvement in that effort. I think he was close to the campus during his service as a senator. When the Voinovich Center was established, he was delighted, and he has been active with the center.

He spent three days last week or so on campus with the center, and he has been good enough to name the Ohio University Libraries as a depository for all his papers: two terms as governor, and extended terms as a senator. He was an important figure as a state legislator and as mayor of Cleveland. It's quite a history, and those papers should make for interesting research material.

George was a man who acted on his own with a sense of what was right. He listened to others but he did what he was convinced was right. He did not necessarily follow a political line. He followed his own sense of need. I could go to him and talk to him, but he would weigh that, in all honesty, against what were the larger needs of other institutions in the state. But he and Janet were always quick to respond to requests to show their loyalty.

We haven't talked about the legislature.

Governor George Voinovich presenting the Governor's Award to President Ping, 1992.

SC: That's what I was trying to formulate in a question. Why don't you just go ahead and talk about what it was like to have to go and testify, who you dealt with regularly, and the changes in your presidency. As you said earlier, Rhodes tended to get along well with the Democratic leaders when it was a split—

CP: Yes.

SC: between the governorship and the legislature. Go ahead and talk about what memories come to mind in terms of having to testify, for instance. Did you—

CP: Well,—

SC: I mean Ohio is an interesting state because each state university does not go before the legislature to lobby for its own budget. There is a formula, but there must be other things that are related to that—

CP: Yes.

SC: that presidents have to go lobby for.

CP: Yes. I had always gone with the president of Central Michigan when he had to testify. This was my introduction to legislative and public university life. I had arrived on the Central Michigan campus with all of my educational experience as a student, as a faculty member, and as an administrator on private campuses. Central was my first public university experience.

President Bill Boyd, whom I had known for years back, and with whom I was very, very close, said to me, "All right, Charlie, in January we have to go," and this was September, "before the legislature and testify. When we go before the legislature, I want you to know the Central Michigan budget so thoroughly, either from your head or from your briefcase, that you pull the answer to any questions that the Appropriations Committee might choose to ask us." Bill was my mentor, and this was part of my crash course.

SC: This is Central Michigan—

CP: That's right.

SC: not Ohio University?

CP: This was my introduction to politics, legislatures, and public universities.

SC: That is that any question could come from anywhere. You couldn't just prepare for one subject.

CP: In Michigan, the Senate Appropriations Committee was the key to whatever budget you had. The Michigan budget was not based on formula; it was strictly institutional pleading. I went fully expecting to be grilled on stewardship of public money. I think that I lost my naiveté in the course of that afternoon. I remember the first question that came. We were in the old Supreme Court chamber, and there was a raised dais. The chairman of the committee leaned forward and said, "Doctor Boyd, I'd like you to answer one question. Is it true that you used a state vehicle to pick up one of the 'Chicago Seven,' who came to campus to speak?" Bill turned to me, and I said, "Probably." [laughs]

SC: [laughs]

CP: And so, and from that point on, the questions went downhill. I was delighted to find that there really was a serious engagement, through the board of regents, in issues related to the fairness of the operating budget of the institutions here.

SC: In Ohio?

CP: In Ohio. It was, in fact, a budget that was so rationally constructed that it was hard to fault the reasoning. It was based upon an analysis of audited financial records, and it was redone periodically in terms of costs of a particular type of course. So a general studies course had a dollar value per one full-time equated student, and a senior course in physics had a different value because of the costs related to each. The issues were cost determined; more pointedly, it is both rational and fair. So, we got absolutely the same dollar amount for a medical school student that Ohio State got. Of course, they got teaching hospital funds because this was part of the history of the medical school there. But it was completely rational, and it was removed, largely, from the political process. And it was fair. It was never adequately funded, but the distribution of funds was fair. You could not really, materially, influence that. When I testified it was "more" for all.

So the hearings were not hearings in terms of institutional hearings, but the board of regents, because they were a planning board of directors, were set up to establish fair recommendations to the legislature. The regents were not a governing board. They were a policy review board. And I think—

SC: Did you have to remind them of that from time to time?

CP: I fought that battle for nineteen years.

SC: [laughs]

CP: [laughs] Nationally, all state coordinating bodies seek to move to become governing bodies. It's only as a result of constant vigilance that institutions are allowed to function freely. Anyhow, the hearings were interesting and typically included the Inter-University Council (IUC), an organization of the presidents and a trustee from every university campus. Then there was a separate organization for the community and technical colleges.

IUC would ask a couple presidents to testify on behalf of the budget. I was asked with some frequency to testify, probably more than was usual, in a biannual cycle. And virtually without exception, the president of Ohio State was asked to testify because it's a key university in the state—

SC: Absolutely.

CP: that is a balanced mix of institutions. The first president of Ohio State that I worked with was a man I grew to admire and—

SC: Was this Harold Enarson?

CP: Yes. He was a political scientist by training.

SC: [Edward H.] Jennings would have been the second.

CP: That's right.

SC: He was an economist. Enarson had been president at Cleveland State before—

CP: Yes, he was. And he was a fine, thoughtful, intellectual man. He was one of a handful of presidents I really related to. He was scrupulously honest, insisting that Ohio State was bound by the state statute that says that all public institutions will accept any applicant, without further testing, based upon their high school graduation diploma. And Ohio State, for years, did that. They accepted, on the order of receipt, graduates of high schools in Ohio. They were later than we in establishing selected admissions. Anyway, Harold Enarson had a dry wit that would hit home if you listened carefully, and he tended to use that wit whether he was in conversation or a formal setting of testifying before the legislature.

In a year that the legislature was seriously cutting budgets, or talking about it, I testified immediately after Harold. He sat down at the witness table, and said, "This is simply going to devastate the institution, and we only have two principal sources of revenue, student tuition and state subsidy; therefore, if you do what's being discussed, we will have to raise tuition by 38 percent." The chairman of the committee said, "Like Hell you will. We will set caps." And that's when that got put in place. We've lived with them most years, ever since. And the cap actually becomes the minimum because you can't afford not to rise to the cap. The figure in the future becomes a percentage of a percentage.

Anyway, when he got through, I testified. I felt like the lamb being led to slaughter, frequently. But you testified, essentially, to the needs of higher education and to the reasonableness of the budget. You did not testify, typically, to the particular needs of institutions, except as they were built into the structure of the budget proposal.

Now the Capital bill was a free-for-all. It was clearly a political process, much to the annoyance of the board of regents. They would offer a Capital bill, and then people would have things inserted. The relation with the board of regents and this campus was strained right from the beginning because they were deeply angered by the fact that the legislature had provided special funding for Ohio University as it tottered on the edge of bankruptcy; they gave us, I've forgotten the figures, somewhere between three to five million, and they said "go solve your problem."

In the same year that they gave Ohio University special funding in spite of vigorous resistance by the board of regents they also created a College of Osteopathic Medicine here, also vigorously resisted by the board of regents. But the political force of the Ohio Osteopathic group was far stronger than the political force of the board of regents. And the college was created; this campus was designated as the site. But those two issues stuck in the craw of the regents, and there were some tense years. While I think there was respect—I certainly had regard for each of the chancellors, some more than others—I was always pleading the case for Ohio University in any conversation. That, sometimes, was at cross-purposes with what the regents wanted.

Let me add this. I think Ohio has a far more rational structure than Michigan. I was pleased to see that structure when I began to study what was already here. Thanks to the first chancellor, John Millett, it's a very carefully designed structure. It is, as I said, coherent, fair, and rational. The two charges to the board of regents are to make recommendations on funding, and to examine any proposals for new campuses, and thus advise the legislature on those issues. I think that they have served the state well as kind of a buffer between the individual institutions. There was no reasonableness to the Michigan budgets. It was a political process and the University of Michigan, frankly, had the muscle.

SC: The first muscle, and Michigan State had the second muscle—

CP: That's right.

SC: and on down the line.

CP: Wayne State third and the rest came along. In Ohio that has not been true. There is not a flagship campus at a cost to other institutions. Clearly, Ohio State is the most comprehensive, and it is certainly the largest university with a complete array of professional schools. That's not true of any other campus; Cincinnati is the exception. Cincinnati came late into the state system and has virtually the same array of programs as Ohio State.

SC: Can you think of any moment when you had to make a case with the regents? Were there times when they wanted to meddle?

CP: Yes, there were a series of times, really, when they began to suggest that this or that ought to be done. I had to act in a way that antagonized some of the chairpersons of the board of regents. But I wasn't going to walk away from the contest, because one of the marvelous things that you have in Ohio is legislatively mandated autonomy. Each of the campuses has its own governing board that is the responsible agent in making basic decisions.

What you have in the board of regents is also an important part of the picture. You have somebody in charge of oversight for the whole of higher education. I think that's a very healthy balance, but there's a continuous push for the regents to move into a governance role. Sometimes it is conscious, and obvious; sometimes it's oblique. Eternal vigilance, as I said a minute ago, is the key to preserving institutional autonomy.

SC: Tell the story that you've shared with me several times about having to testify before the legislature. I don't know what the issue was, but the question of autonomy and funding got linked, and a legislator made a famous reply to you when you were holding out for autonomy.

CP: I was presenting an eloquent case, I thought, for the autonomy of institutions. And the chairman of the committee got a little impatient with it because it didn't really interest him. So he said, "Mr. Ping, there's one lesson you need to learn. You can't eat autonomy." [laughs]

SC: Do you remember any legislative leaders with a particular fondness, or with a particular pain?

CP: Well, I was very fond of, and very close to, Vern Riffe, who held the interests of Southern Ohio close. He was a good friend of Ohio University. He was also a good person. We talked, at first privately. He was a political leader of the old school, but the term limits have ended the possibility of Vern Riffes. When he made a decision, it was usually going to happen because he had good discipline within the party caucus, and if somebody got out of line, he got even. Things happened because of Vern.

I was an active advocate, when it was proposed, for the concept of term limits. I've now seen the consequence of term limits, and I'm no longer so sure that it's a good thing. Because what it means is that, with a limited number of terms, state government becomes more British in character, the administration and the unelected bureaucrats behind the scenes become too influential. A legislator takes a couple of sessions to be able to understand something as complicated as a formula funding.

SC: How it works.

CP: Even people in the higher education business, with this as their special interest, take years to get inside the funding models and to really understand how institutions get their dollars. Vern was always quick to call if there was something that concerned him.

One of my favorite faculty members is a Distinguished Professor in Economics, now emeritus, Rich Vedder. Rich is prone to a contrary point of view on most issues, and he writes with well-documented arguments on everything from how Walmart is economically an asset to a community, to how schools really are not improved with more funds. He wrote a series of op-ed pieces that appeared in newspapers around the state when the legislature was trying earnestly to increase funding for public schools. Vern Riffe was one of the leaders in this whole effort.

SC: Yes.

CP: Out of the blue, Vern called me and said, "Charlie, can't you do something about that G—D— economist on your faculty?" And I said, "Not really." And he said, "Can't you stop him from writing these pieces?"

Distinguished Professor of Economics Richard K. Vedder, ca. 1986.

And I said, "I can certainly try to persuade him, but I can't stop him from writing." He said, "Well he's costing us." Rich was providing evidence that at the schools that were less well-funded, the performance of the students on any of the well-accepted measures was better; the real variable, he insisted, was a household that was with two parents and so on. There are a whole host of characters that I look back on with some fondness in the legislature. Vern tops the list.

I don't look back with great fondness on regular trips to Columbus. In fact, they became a drain. When I had had the bilateral knee implants and a lot of other orthopedic problems, I decided that I had neither the energy nor the patience for the job. I found myself listening to some student group with an argument for the first twenty or thirty minutes, and finally saying, "You know, that's a lot of nonsense, and you're wasting your time and my time." That's not a smart thing to do. A president has to listen until the end, nod, and then get rid of them.

I found myself saying to political leadership, "You know, instead of blaming each other, Democrats or Republicans, you ought to act to address the problem. We need a decision on the budget." That's a summary of a conversation with George Voinovich. That's not a smart thing to say to a governor. They know that—

SC: [laughs] They don't appreciate—

CP: That's right. And, you know, I sort of reached my end point. Anyhow, the long and the short of it is this: only three times in my two decades did I listen to the call of other institutions. I had many invitations, but I only agreed to be a candidate at Michigan State and some years later at Oregon State. Michigan State because I had a lot of friends on the faculty there, some friends within their governing board, and knew many of the key members of the legislature. I admire Michigan State as the model land grant college. And that interested me greatly. Oregon State interested me because of the beauty of the area and the strength of the institution. But in the end, I decided "No" in both cases.

SC: I remember Ocasek was quoted in the paper. Oliver Ocasek was, I think, one of the leaders, if not the leader of the Senate.

CP: He was president of the Senate.

SC: He said that when Michigan State called him, to ask about you, he said, "They could have any five Ohio presidents, but they couldn't have you." [laughs]

CP: [laughs] And I remember what you said. Do you remember what you said?

SC: No.

CP: I can't believe that—

SC: Oh.

CP: "Anyone who has been an Athenian would hardly choose to be a Spartan." [laughs] Anyway, the point of the story, really, was dealing with the legislature. In the end, I told the chairman that I really was not going to be a candidate at Michigan State.

I came to the same decision about Oregon State. The Willamette Valley is such a lovely area, and Oregon State is such an interesting land grant institution, but it is tremendously impoverished by the lack of state funding. Yet it is attracting and holding one of the best faculties in the country. That's intriguing.

SC: The connection being: That what ultimately you weren't interested in doing was having to deal with the legislature on a regular basis.

CP: Yes, the third time I agreed to be a candidate was with a major private university. Private university presidents do not, generally, deal with state legislators. I remember being greatly tempted, and I don't know what I would have decided. It ended up that I was one of the two finalists, and, I think, they wisely chose the other person.

SC: Charlie, I think that's a good stopping place for today.

CONVERSATION
with
SAM CROWL

May 31, 2011

SC: Charlie, Ohio University, though it's a national university and has a place on the national stage, has had a particular responsibility to the area in Southeastern Ohio, which gives us our place and our life. Could you talk a bit about the relationship of your administration to the regional campus system that rings Athens? Then go on to talk about the ways in which your administration tried to be helpful in the economic development in the region?

CP: Well, I think that a university is in a particular place and a particular time; both place and time deliver imperatives. This University has a particular obligation to Southeastern Ohio. In a very special way, with the ring of regional campuses from the Eastern campus up by Wheeling and all the way to the Ironton campus, or as they prefer, the Southern campus, Ohio University has an important role in providing educational access for people, particularly for people whose work or family responsibilities constrain their access. The average age of the students on the regional campuses is older. There are many people who are stepping in and out of their educational experience, and I think it's an important service we offer.

Sometime in the '80s, I asked for a study. At that point in time, half the students enrolled in all of Ohio higher education with home addresses and zip codes from this area were enrolled in Ohio University, both the main and regional campuses. And I tried consciously to integrate the regional campuses into the main campus. We had exceptional leadership at the regional campuses in Jim Bryant, and a whole succession of very able deans at the campuses. While, I think, in '75, there was some resistance because of the turmoil in Athens, gradually they were won over, and they saw their association with Ohio University as being an important asset.

I think we worked and tried to build an ease of movement from the regional campus into the main campus. Students might begin a degree on the regional campus but finish it on the main campus.

We also began an effort to move out to the regional campuses degrees that were needed in the area, with the idea that we would be there for a period of time until the need was met. For example, in the specialized areas in education, there might be a backlog of teachers who needed a master's degree. So we moved faculty back and forth to the regional campuses. We also tried to get regional campuses more into the minds of the trustees by regularly scheduling one of the four stated meetings each year on regional campuses. And I think this became an important event at each of the campuses. All in all, I think we built a network that served the needs of education well.

We were very conscious of the fact that this region is an economically depressed region, and it is in desperate need of jobs. As the extractive industries began to lay off tens and then hundreds of thousands of people, there was a great void in the region. Through a variety of means such as the retraining of people on the regional campus, through the Innovation Center, we tried to help. Thanks to the good work of Will Konneker and a whole group of people. Alan Geiger in his role as campus planner, both for the regional campuses and the main campus, was another important factor. And we had some enterprising deans on these campuses.

Bill Dingus at Ironton was a classic example. He actively promoted that campus and was successful in a remarkable way. My first visit to the Ironton campus, I went down there my first year for a high school football game when my son was a senior in high school; I went early to visit our Ironton campus. Our campus, at that time, consisted of two classrooms in the Ironton High School with a library in one of the rooms. That was it. Before Bill Dingus retired, Ironton was an elaborate campus with a whole set of new facilities. It had a role in the community that easily translated into progress. When Bill resigned, he moved into economic development for Lawrence County and for the whole area.

SC: Those are interesting jobs, the regional campus deans, because they're educational entrepreneurs. You find ways of meeting the needs of the community, which may not be consistent over time. You're like a little president because you are the representative of the University and the campus in that community, and the academic leader. It's a job that has many hats.

CP: Yes, and community relations is an essential part of the role. Each of the campuses, of course, has its own regional council appointed by the board of trustees, and part of the dean's role is, in fact, to find ways to relate the campus to the community.

SC: How did you manage to walk through the natural tension that exists between the main campus and the regional campuses? At least in the time that I served in administration, there was a constant drumbeat to and from the regional campuses, to have four-year programs, and to offer permanent degrees, not just one that might come for a while to meet a need and move away. Will you talk a bit about how we tried to handle that or manage it?

CP: Well, it was always a conscious push. Wherever possible, we tried to staff the need with faculty who were teaching in Athens, but who were willing to drive to the regional campuses to provide some supplement for the faculty there. When the campus had qualified faculty, they taught. We were really trying to help them offer some of the degree work, at least in four-year programs in areas where there was a very strong interest. In business, for example, and in education we began to get regional campus—

based programs. The key was always to maintain a high level of expectation and quality related to a baccalaureate program.

SC: It was also true that the regional campuses could be more responsive to retraining efforts in moments of economic downturn.

CP: Yes, because they clearly had access to the people who needed retraining. I think the Eastern campus and the Southern campus did particularly fine jobs in this area. Each of the campuses was conscious of this as an imperative throughout the whole region, a region troubled by a steady decline in jobs.

SC: Could you talk a bit about the development? I'm going to have to confess that I have a breakdown in name here. What is the name of the regional institute that we established here that's now called the Voinovich School of Leadership and Public Affairs, and it attempted to reach out to communities in this area to aid them in, I think, problems of governance and managing infrastructure and economic development?

CP: Well, it was a dream and vision of a political science professor—

SC: Mark Weinberg.

CP: Mark Weinberg, and it was originally called ILGARD—Institute for Local Government Administration and Rural Development. Mark was tireless in trying to provide expertise and assistance to the communities throughout the region. He built a remarkable base that has flowered now into the Voinovich School of Leadership and Public Affairs. I think that it has a great future for training people for public service and for providing professional consultation to local communities.

SC: That brings me to another local subject. Maybe we'll start here, and then move on to Athens, which is the downtown community. Secondarily, the ILGARD, and now the Voinovich School, is located on the Ridges,

Mark Weinberg, the
founder of the Institute
for Local Government
Administration and
Rural Development
(ILGARD), at a class-
room podium, 1987.

which is what the collection of buildings came to be called that were
once a part of the State Mental Health Hospital.

Take us through your relationship with Governor Celeste in Columbus concerning the long-standing mental health institute, which once, I
think, probably housed three thousand patients, but had shrunk greatly.
Although it was a vast physical plant, there was a new hospital built next
to O'Bleness, along the other side of the river. The problem was what to
do with the Victorian buildings.

CP: Well, it became obvious that the facilities were going to be abandoned, together with about 800 acres of land. Of that total, only something like 26, already crowded with buildings, was suited for building.

The rest was slip prone. So we had a lot of land, and a lot of liabilities: cemeteries and buildings that had been abandoned for years. They essentially just nailed the doors shut and walked away from them. Some of them had been abandoned for decades.

Ora Anderson and his wife saw possibilities in the Dairy Barn. I went out with Ora and Harriet, his wife, to the Dairy Barn. Ora waxed eloquently about what this facility might mean as an art center for the community, but all I could see, looking around me, were the cow stalls. The leavings of cows that were still very much in evidence, and the building represented a tremendous cost—but what a beautiful area of brick courtyard surrounding it. Anyway, the Andersons and the Athens community did, in fact, carry out that dream, and the Dairy Barn has been such an asset to the area.

SC: Yes, I think Ora Anderson got to Governor Rhodes as the wrecking ball was very close to closing in—

CP: Yes.

SC: on the Dairy Barn to, in fact, save it for the very purpose that it has served so well.

CP: I don't think they were going to tear it down. I think that they were just going to abandon it as they had with most of the buildings up there; it had actually stood for some time as an abandoned building. Then the issue was this huge block of land. There was a local group who wanted to keep the Ridges from the clutches of the University or a developer. Ora was the leader. They were looking for some way to finance a development up there, initially a retirement community.

Unfortunately, none of it made much economic sense, and Ora was prudent enough to see this clearly. He came to me and said, "All right, this is really a heritage, and we need to preserve it. The University is the only entity in the community that has the resources to do it. Would you please see that it is turned over to the University?"

Claire and I, for the next several months, spent our Sunday afternoons walking the grounds, lovely grounds. Much of it is very hilly. Some of it had been farmed, and some just in trees and brush; there are a lot of lovely sites up there. Even the old buildings, some of them—not all of them—had a grace and dignity. Claire is a preservation enthusiast; I share some of her interests and concerns. But as we walked, all I could see was an endless outgo of money. If we took these 700-and-some-odd acres, the immediate cost to the University, still struggling with budget issues, would be millions, literally. You'd have to have an expanded police force, and you'd have to have a refurbished heating plant. We'd have to worry with all the issues of taking it over, including all these cemeteries that we'd be obligated to maintain. But over time, I began to see that the potential was great.

So with the trustees' support we sought both legislative action and the governor's support for the transfer of the land to the trustees of Ohio University for the use and benefit of the University. And the land was so transferred. Then we hired an architectural firm to study each of the buildings standing up there, and to rank them in order of desirability in terms of whether or not they could be converted and put to other purposes. We soon discovered that some of the old hospital's main building had been completely redone, and it had been used as a hospital. So it was clearly up to code. But we also discovered a whole series of issues in other buildings, everything from concrete that would crumble if you cut into it, to asbestos. The first building that seemed, in terms of cost benefit analysis, to make sense was, in fact, the old auditorium.

SC: A lovely little Greek Revival temple.

CP: And it was restored and converted into usable performance space and other purposes.

SC: And it had the advantage of getting people up on the Ridges who had never been there before to come to the performances.

CP: We had been given this magnificent collection by Ed Kennedy, which was justly described as the world's finest collection of Navaho weaving; a superb set of pieces of Indian jewelry that Ed had commissioned as gifts for his wife; and many pieces of flatware, all done by the Navahos. We had the world's only complete collection of Navaho prayer cycle rugs; they, like Navaho sand paintings, were never complete in every detail. But we had seven cycles.

Here we were with this extraordinary collection. I went to Governor Celeste, and said, "We have a world-class collection that people will literally come to Athens just to see this collection." Ed's insistent theme: he intended and hoped that it would be a working collection.

SC: When did the idea come for using the main building of the main hospital for a museum? We'd been talking about a museum for a long time—

CP: Yes.

SC: and there had been other ideas—

CP: Yes. Well, we tried to raise funds for it in the 1804 Campaign. Henry Lin, who was the dean of fine arts, thought that this would be something that people would be quick to support. We could not find anyone to contribute a major gift. So it was one of the unmet goals of the 1804 Campaign. We did get support from the state in the Capital bill. It was the first time that the state put money into a museum. Governor Celeste, I think, recognized the possibilities. Schoolchildren would be pouring in; they would be bussed to see this. Anyway, now the University had the money for a museum. What do we do with it?

The first building chosen was the site of the old post office that housed the economics department at the time.

SC: Do you mean Haning Hall?

CP: Haning Hall. That was where we were going to put the museum, and we worked at some length to figure this out. Ed, as part of the planning committee, said, "You're just not gonna have enough space to provide the appropriate storage as well as a display area." And somebody else said, "Plus that's an impossible place—"

SC: To park?

CP: "to park or take school buses to in any number," and, "Where are they going to unload the students?" So we began to look around, and the next idea was the main building of the Ridges—the center tower part of the building. I was a little skeptical because I wasn't particularly drawn to the building. The architectural beauty of the building escaped me, but it had character. It was, I think, a typical mental health facility of the late nineteenth century. We settled on it because it had parking and worlds of space.

We took the money that had been appropriated and started the task of converting it. Very quickly we discovered that the cost of converting that space was going to be significantly higher than originally estimated. So we had to do it in stages. But much to everyone's delight, the first floor turned out to be a superb museum space—very high ceilings and large expanses of wall. It has all the characteristics of a good museum. And we were able to build into the building, at considerable expense, storage space to preserve this fine collection, and whatever else might come. The museum has won steadily increasing support and interest. It is a marvelous asset to the campus.

SC: And it carries the names of the key figures you've been talking about. The museum is named after Ed and Ruth Kennedy, alumni of the University who gave the collection. And Henry Lin, who was the dean of fine arts when all this began to take shape—I believe the building itself is called Lin Hall.

CP: Yes.

SC: We probably should include here a little bit for those who do not know about Henry's very accomplished daughter. Henry and Julia—I should say his wife, Julia, was a very distinguished critic of contemporary Chinese poetry and was a longtime member of the English department —had a remarkable daughter, and she is, of course,—

CP: Maya Lin, who as a very young architect, just finishing college, submitted the winning design for the Vietnam War Memorial. Henry was a very accomplished ceramist, as well, and he did some magnificent pieces. When I retired, Julia presented Claire and me with a piece of Henry's work that was featured on the catalogue published for a show of Henry's work.

   Julia and I put Henry's ashes under a flowering tree planted in front of Trisolini. Julia has remained active as a scholar publishing contemporary Chinese female poets in the last few years, and she is now working on an autobiography.

SC: They were a remarkable family. And Henry was a remarkable dean.

CP: Yes, he was sort of stubborn and strong willed. I remember when he retired, and we were appointing a new dean. I said, "Henry, where will you work?" And he said to me, "Where are you going to put the new dean?" [laughs]

SC: [laughs]

CP: And I said, "Well, I assume in Trisolini." He said, "Not in my office."

SC: [laughs]

CP: And I thought about it, and I decided it was easier to do a new office for the dean than to move Henry Lin. [laughs]

SC: Charlie, when you arrived, besides the University being in trouble, the town was going through a transformation. First, shopping malls had been built on East State Street where the automobile dealerships were, and the downtown was undergoing a transformation. It had been the commercial center of Athens for all its life. There were department stores, shoe stores, and what have you, and that's where people came to do their shopping on Saturday. But that was gradually changing. Then, early on in your administration, there were a series of very bad fires that gutted a number of the buildings. What sort of a role did you try to play, either up front or behind the scenes, in terms of revitalizing downtown Athens and helping it make the transition to being primarily a commercial area that serves the students?

CP: Well, I give a great deal of credit to Claire and a group of women who came together to form a preservation group. They were instrumental in a series of awards that were presented to store owners, who were willing to bear the expense and effort to restore a building. I regularly met with the downtown merchants and tried to help them. But the handwriting was on the wall. The downtown area was becoming a center for student businesses and that meant fast food and bars and a whole lot of other things.

SC: Bookstores, college shops—

CP: Sure.

SC: Ice cream stores.

CP: Drugstores and things that students would patronize. And sadly, gradually, virtually all the clothing stores closed—the reasons for local people to go downtown disappeared over time. The University really was the first developer of the mall. There was a need for more grocery stores. Kroger was the principal leaser of land, and that lease returned handsome dividends to the University. I think all who wanted to save the downtown as it once was, simply came to realize that it wasn't going to be. But there were people like Les Cornwell and others who really took delight in trying to—as they built student-oriented facilities—to preserve something of the original character. The brick streets were preserved at the insistence of this group of women and others, and I think downtown Athens has its own distinct character.

SC: Obviously, determining to keep the architectural integrity of a place is not something that happens by accident. People have to determine that what is there has value; this is a part of what, beyond the University, makes Athens unique. We often forget, but it's a very charming downtown, and it is well maintained.

For a better part of a decade, a lot of it was boarded up as we waited to restore buildings from those devastating fires. How much of a help was your relationship with Tad Grover? He comes from a family that has been long connected to the University.

CP: Tad and the banks: The Athens National Bank, Bank One and now Chase, particularly when it was Athens National and Bank One, were clearly locally oriented and eager to see that the community and its several small businesses prosper. I don't have any direct knowledge of the '60s here, but Tad served as a link between city council and those businesses, and later, as a trustee of the University, between the campus and the community. During the very difficult years of the '60s, he was for eight or ten years on the city council, and he was a key banker in providing the loans that sustained and helped the businesses develop. I think the truth of the matter is that it all goes back to John C. Baker.

Dr. Baker arrived on the scene in 1945. Cutler Hall, the central building of the campus, had fallen into such disrepair that the state architect was insisting that it be torn down. John, who came from Harvard to Ohio University, had a real sense of history. Cutler is the oldest building on any campus in the old Northwest Territory, and it's a handsome old structure. John was a very stubborn man, and he fought the state architect on this issue tooth and nail. The state architect even said, "All right, we'll tear it down and build a building that is an exact replica." And John would have no part of that. He wanted the building restored. Much to everyone's gain, John won the fight.

The very costly process of restoring those hand-pressed bricks that were porous and covered by countless layers of paint was part of the

Historic Cutler Hall as seen from the College Green, 1979.

expense. I think John's sense of history began to permeate the whole community. It carried over to Court Street. The college and the town are a whole—they are parts of an historical legacy. Cutler, and the two buildings that flank it, provided the key.

SC: Yes, and there was, you know, no greater treat that both of us had, at various times, than to walk the campus with John pointing out everything from trees to the mortar between the bricks in Bryan Hall, and the technique that made that mortar look like it was 150 years old, rather than 50 years old or 60 years old. He was someone who didn't believe that things wore out. He'd say to me, "What are you going to tear down that building for? That's a perfectly good building."

CP: [laughs]

SC: [laughs]

CP: We were in the process of building the new Aquatic Center. I was with him, and we were talking about this and that—what's going on on the campus—and I said, "We're building a new Aquatic Center." He said, "What? We just built one!" It was decades old by this time and entirely inadequate for the University. [laughs]

SC: [laughs] Speak a bit about how valuable—you've mentioned his role as university planner, the campus planning and space and all that goes with it—how valuable Alan Geiger was to you in dealing with community relations and keeping tabs with city council, and even, I suppose, relationships in Columbus over the years.

CP: Yes. Well, the University was well served by a whole set of people, and I certainly was well served by several people integral to that office. Marie White was a secretary and an administrative assistant for five presidents of Ohio University—John Baker, Vern Alden, Claude Sowle,—

SC: Harry Crewson.

CP: Harry Crewson, and me. Five very different people, yet all of them felt that she was indispensable. She was unflappable, no matter how demanding students, or alumni, or whatever the group. But somehow she

Formal portrait of Ohio University presidents with Marie White on the occasion of her retirement. Marie White was the very able administrative assistant and senior secretary for all four presidents in the picture: (*left to right*) Dr. Ping, Dr. Baker, Dr. Crewson, and Dr. Alden stand behind a seated Marie White, 1993.

never seemed to be troubled by these kinds of demands, and she was always infinitely patient and infinitely discreet with all of her presidents.

SC: Yes, it's her oral history that I'd really like to have. [laughs] But she's too discreet to talk—

(*Left to right*) President Ping with Robert Mahn and Alan Geiger in front of the Robert E. Mahn Reading Room in Alden Library's Archives & Special Collections, 1984. Robert Mahn retired as assistant to the president and secretary of the board of trustees after almost fifty years of faithful service. Alan Geiger was his successor.

CP: [laughs] That's one oral history that John Baker said can never be published. And then there was Bob Mahn, who for almost fifty years served the University in a variety of roles. He had been the secretary of the University; he was meticulous as the secretary to the board of trustees in keeping the record of the University. And Marty Hecht was the legislative liaison officer, who in addition to moving the river, had a whole list of major projects. He had been integral, and he had the ear of key legislators in Columbus and Washington. When Bob Mahn retired, I needed someone as an assistant. We also needed someone as legislative liaison when Marty Hecht retired. Alan was brought into the office.

I had learned to have great confidence in his work with campus planning. And in that role, because the Capital bill is so politicized, he had built good relations with legislators and other officials in Columbus.

He had to get funds released from state committees and to reinforce the value of ideas for capital projects. He is the sort of person who works well with widely different groups of people. Alan was a key person in quietly building strong relationships with city government, the community at large, and the state legislature. He was invaluable. He was the man who would solve a problem, and you'd never even know it. He was immensely helpful to Claire as well.

SC: I'm going to make a little segue here. Ohio University was the first campus in the state system to have at least a portion of the nonacademic workers unionize. It happened in President Alden's years, and then every three years from the first quasi-strike to a positive union vote, when the contract came up for renewal there'd be the threat of a strike. I remember in the third year I was here there was a strike of about two weeks' time. I think in maybe the second or third year that you were president, it was time for a contract renewal. There was a strike. There has not been one since, in thirty-five years. Talk a bit about how you addressed the relationship with AFSCME, which was the local union, and how you managed to create, or how your administration created, the context for successful bargaining.

CP: First of all, in 1975, there was a strong feeling of ill will because a great many people had to be laid off to address the budget crisis. Over a hundred, I don't remember the exact number of people in the support staff, had lost their jobs. The residence halls were 40 percent empty, so staff shrunk and there was a strong climate of resentment over that fact. Plus in the external environment the United Mine Workers had been out for two months as our contract with AFSCME was coming up for renewal. One of the things that I discovered is that the United Mine Workers is not just a union: it's a way of life and a way of thinking. That whole mind-set was very strong throughout this region. There was a kind of manhood issue, which was to be as brave as the mine workers.

So, all the conditions were ripe for a strike, and in 1978, we did have a strike. It lasted around two weeks. We had carefully prepared. We had

Striking members of the American Federation of State, County and Municipal Employees (AFSCME) Local 1699 sharing a hot beverage on the East Green picket line, 1978.

identified issues that we were prepared to take a strike for and issues that, if they didn't get, we thought they would strike. We'd been through this analysis, and Neil Bucklew was trained in labor relations, and I had some experience with collective bargaining. Most importantly, the key people like Chuck Culp, Bob Hynes, Bill Kennard, and a whole lot of other people, were thoroughly prepared. It was a surprise when they actually went out because there really wasn't a strike issue on the table. The strike dragged on, day after day, and it had its ugly moments. We had to move coal onto the campus using armed guards against the threat of disruption.

SC: There's a certain irony in that, but we'll let that go.

CP: Well, we had to go some distance to—

SC: No, but coal and the miners and the tradition of the area—

CP: I was puzzled by this whole scene; I couldn't make sense out of it. One day I went down to the Convo—I used to work out there—and one of the men who worked in the Convo, with whom I was friends, was manning the barrel on the picket line. As I went by him, I looked at him and said, "How about walking down the road with me? You know, I'm so worried; I'd like to understand—why are you on strike? What's going on?" And he said, "Mr. Ping, I don't have any idea why we're on strike. But let me tell ya somethin'." He said, "My father could not open nor close either hand because he had been holding the gate when the strike breakers hit the mine, and they broke every bone in both his hands before he let go. So if the union says 'go out,' I'll go out." Well, that's a little hard to deal with.

We managed to continue to function with the vital services and instruction by a simple device. We issued a check that was equal to the day's payment for food to every student in the residence halls. Bill Kennard was the architect, the treasurer, behind all this, and he and his staff brought it to pass. As you can imagine, it was a very large undertaking. So we doled out these checks, but the checks were—I don't remember—about $1.75 or some ridiculously small sum. I got calls from parents who said, "How do you expect my child to eat?" I would reply, "Well, that's what it costs and that's what you paid;—that's how we figured the reimbursement."

Anyhow, sadly, during that period my father died. So the family and I drove to Florida in a tense period. I would stop and call twice in the morning, twice in the afternoon, and again in the evening to talk with Neil about the progress. And after two weeks out, it was apparent, I think, to everyone that we needed to end this. It was doing harm to the University, and that meant, potentially, the loss of more jobs. I think the union began to recognize that, and we settled, ending the strike. We gathered a group of people who were directly responsible for labor relations. Chuck Culp was a key person, and others working with him, to begin building a different relation. It did not have to be—

SC: Necessarily—

CP: adversarial. Why could we not, in fact, walk, work, and talk together. Carol Harter later provided much-needed leadership to this effort. It took years and years, but we began to build better working relationships and a trust. I think that there was, by the early 1990s, a good understanding. There's still clearly a difference in interests; these are sometimes contentious, but there's also, I think, thanks to the leadership in the University and in the union, to Charlie Adkins, and to his successors—

SC: Tommy [Adkins] before Charlie.

CP: Tommy, yes, Tommy before Charlie, and working together was in their best interest and in all our best interest. In fact, it was so pronounced that good relations are one of the things that I cherish.

As I was retiring, it was decided that they would put the Office of the President Emeritus in Henry Lin's old office in Trisolini. The building has seen a lot of use over the years. It served John Baker and his family as a presidential residence. The physical plant undertook a major renovation of the building. In the process, they had to redo the heat and air conditioning. One of the things that they determined that they would do as a special touch, knowing how I had enjoyed the fireplace and how I'd use the fireplace in my office in Cutler, they added a project to completely redo the fireplace that is in my office now. They brought in chimney sweeps and rebuilt it to safety standards, so that it was possible to have a fire in that fireplace. What a lovely thing to do. I was deeply appreciative of the fact that they were support staff of the campus. They had called for the redo. Unfortunately, in that old building, I've never had the courage to—

SC: I was going to say, [laughs]

CP: [laughs]

SC: I did remember the fire going in your office in Cutler, but I'm right not to remember any going in Trisolini.

CP: Well, I think, the issue was a basic trust, so that we were trying to bargain not just to the crisis of the moment but continuously. While we have differences, we also have some common interests. Some very extra-ordinary effort went into this. I can't begin to name all the people, on both sides of the table, who contributed to it, but a great many people did.

SC: It must be rather unusual when the management of an institution hires the labor negotiator for the union, Fred Haynes, to be its negotia-tor. That worked, and I would have thought there would have been a tension about all that, but obviously, that was a trust issue again where the union trusted—

CP: He was a critical part in building that relationship of trust and confidence.

SC: Well, the tradition lives.

CP: Yes.

SC: It's now gone through two administrations, and knock on wood, no strikes.
      We touched on this because of talking about the Ridges and talking about downtown Athens, but let's come back to the campus. You can have a sense of looking back and saying, "There's my legacy out there in many new buildings." But you seemed to be determined to restore when-ever possible. And it was only when you were in a desperate circum-stance, i.e., the Natatorium we needed to replace, that you were willing to think about building new. Is that a matter of looking at the campus and then saying we want to preserve as much of this as possible? Was it Claire and her interest in preservation? Was it your own sense of history? Where did that come from?

CP: Well, it was all of the above, is the simple answer. I think this cam-pus has a legacy, a legacy that is very unique in the Midwest. It has, as you walk the campus, a sense of history. And over the years the president and the trustees have had the good sense to try to preserve that, so that buildings built over the years had some of the same characteristics of the Georgian collegiate architecture that originally marked the campus. I think it's a wonderful legacy. Others argue that campuses ought to reflect different eras, but I disagree. I think there's something about this campus that is very special because of that continuity. Plus it just made good sense.

One of the selling cards that was used to get the medical school here is that we had a lot of space that was unused and still usable. So we began to take buildings off line and remove them from the debt pool and to redo them. Grosvenor Hall was the first unit in the medical school. We would not have been able to build that building from scratch given the time and money available, but all the basic services—the plumbing, the electricity, and all of this was already in the building.

As I said earlier, because of the kitchen area, we had the beginning of a gross anatomy lab, and small cubicle spaces that could be used for offices. Admittedly, it had some disadvantages, too. But we were able, at a saving of—Gerald Faverman did the estimation—something like a third less cost to create usable space. And we took other buildings for the medical school.

Later, we took a dormitory to transform into what is now the home of the Russ College of Engineering, a building appropriately renamed for the Stockers, Paul and Beth Stocker. Again it entailed a significant dollar savings because we had the foundation, we had the basic utilities —everything basic was there. And though we gutted the building, the basic structure was left in place.

Sometimes, it just wasn't sensible. Howard Hall was the first such building to go down. Super Hall went down when it was determined the building had more corridor space than square feet of usable space. It was the most expensive building on campus to operate.

SC: But I think I remember you saying that you regretted taking Super Hall down and that you would never take a building down again that was serviceable.

CP: When you looked at the economic reality, it made sense. It had more space in halls and stairwells than it did in classrooms. But I did regret it because I thought it was a rather handsome—

SC: It seemed to me that we were under some pressure—you were more aware of this than the rest of us—from the board of regents about being "over-spaced." We used to say, "No, we're just under-studented."

CP: [laughs]

SC: But you must have had to fight some battles when you were being pressed to take down even more space.

CP: Well, the basic posture of the chancellor who was in office when I came, and the next chancellor, was that Ohio University would not get a building in the Capital bill until the University reduced by 25 percent the space that we were operating.

SC: So, blackmail.

CP: Pardon?

SC: [laughs] Blackmail.

CP: Yes. Well, we managed to get buildings in the Capital bill anyway. But, it was clearly a continuous battle. Their argument was that we needed to tear down buildings because space was expensive, if we are not actively using it. And I didn't want to tear down; I wanted to build the University.

SC: You also were much taken with ideas of buildings that could be multi-use. I think back to the fact that the Natatorium was really the only major addition to the athletic building on the campus, except for a renovation of Peden Stadium, which expanded its size by putting new seats in the north end zone and by building the tower. The tower was unusual in that, once again, you had the notion that it would be used, not just on football weekends, but it would be used every day of the week.

CP: Yes, yes.

SC: Talk about that and talk about where the model for that came from.

CP: Well, in it were rooms that were to serve as instructional space and tutoring space, all designed to enhance the graduation rate of our student athletes. In fact, we were so much caught up in it that Claire and I donated a painting that we had bought from the widow of one of our campus artists. He had done a series of studies of football players in motion. We gave it as a gift to the tower structural space.

SC: And the notion would be that some of the spaces would be converted on home football weekends to the press box and seating—

CP: We could use some of the space for entertaining guests, including alumni particularly interested in athletics. We had brunches before the game, and it worked well. There was a large, open space that we could use for this purpose, and the football coach could use for team meetings.

SC: And was not the model for this a similar facility at Duke? I seem to recall that you took, in fact, a group of Ohio University followers, maybe members of the board, to the Duke campus to look at the way in which some of their facilities were configured.

CP: Yes. In fact, we didn't really copy their model. Their model combined medical school operations and athletic operations in some interesting ways, and it was a magnificent facility. It was also a very costly facility. But we did, as you mentioned, go around and visit facilities, as we went to play various teams.

I remember visiting South Carolina. They had built a large complex that served only athletics. They had managed to create a separate world for the athletes on campus, so that they lived, ate, and essentially were isolated from the university in much of their daily life. Duke was a better model, in that they had the football team and other athletes live and eat in the residence halls.

SC: Can you think of any other campuses that you looked at when you were thinking about adding here, or thinking about a way in which you wanted to do things here?

CP: Well, we looked at swimming pools on a number of campuses because of a gift from the Nationwide Foundation, thanks to the influence of Dean Jeffers and some of the officials of Nationwide, as well as my service on the board of directors. We had the money to have an architectural competition for the new Aquatic Center. So I went around looking at some attractive buildings. Those who were actively planning the Aquatic Center did more visits because we really wanted a facility that would serve the campus as a recreational facility as well as athletic competition, and one that could conceivably serve the larger community in some direct ways, like swimming classes. We built what I think is a very handsome and usable Aquatic Center with a distinctive roof, one that would not rust.

SC: Let's turn and talk a bit about athletics, particularly intercollegiate athletics. You were a former high school and college football player, and you're someone who is an interested spectator of most of the major spectator sports. You had written about the place of athletics on the campus in the *Chronicle of Higher Education.* How did you try in your own administration to balance the relationship between athletics and the academic side of the University? And what did you see as their potential interaction or their potential synergy?

CP: Well, I had not only played at the high school and college level, I also coached at both the high school and college levels. And frankly, I enjoy athletics. Football was my principal sport and interest. Once president, I tried to ensure that the people who would lead the program, the athletic directors and the coaches, understood that we were primarily a university, and that the athletic program was an integral part of the educational program of the University. So I would interview each of the candidates for head coach, and I would grill them pretty hard and look at their record. But the litmus test, for me, was always "If my son were back in his college days, is this a man whom I would be pleased to have my son play under?" Too many college coaches in today's world are willing to use the athlete to serve their own purpose, and ignore their potential to contribute to the development of students. I also made it a point to show interest. The Athletic Directors Bill Rohr and—

SC: Harold McElhaney.

CP: Yes, Harold McElhaney. We became friends and I think both men understood my insistence. I made a point of going into the locker room after most games, win or lose, and say something to the coach and the team, particularly football and basketball. Joe Carbone and the baseball team were dear to my heart. Joe Carbone was a coach with all the right values in terms of concern for the development of the players, and he stayed with his University.

It occurred to me, as intercollegiate football began to expand the season, that you were bringing eighteen- and nineteen-year-old young people on campus who had been heavily recruited. They were practicing, and even playing one or two ball games before they had ever gone to class. They are supposed to understand that their primary relation is the relation of the student to a university? So I asked the head football coach, and he agreed to have me come down early in the preseason practice and meet with the team. When I did, I would say to them, "Your primary relation is the relationship of a student to a university, and there is an expectation that goes with that. There is one code of student conduct, and there is no exclusion of athletes in this code of conduct." I'm sure that they mostly thought, "Who in the world?" [laughs]

President Ping at one of his signature breakfasts with Ohio University athletes in the presidential residence, 1988.

SC: Who's he kidding. [laughs]

CP: I was no longer big enough to impress them. The world had changed in that way, too. Anyway, I—

SC: What did you try to do to bridge that gap? Did you find some way to have the kids who made the Dean's List to the house for lunch or breakfast or—

CP: Every quarter, we had all the athletes who had better than a 3.5 average in the previous quarter in our home for breakfast. I'd go around the table, and I'd ask each of them to describe their aspirations and major field of study. I got to know a wonderful group of young people.

   I also took an active role in the NCAA, which proved to be, finally, disappointing. But we were, at least, instrumental—a whole large group of us—in establishing a President's Council and to begin to build academic expectation that meant something in the eligibility requirements. Instead of taking a whole set of first-year courses in the junior and senior year, all intercollegiate athletes must now be making reasonable progress toward a degree in a particular program. And, modest though the requirements were, they had to submit test scores and high school performance records that at least held out the expectation that they were going to have some success in college. So I think that's good; it's progress. I don't think it has even begun to scratch the surface, because money in intercollegiate athletics has become dominant.

SC: Sure.

CP: It is, in fact, calling the shots and driving the whole—

SC: Television is one of the major—

CP: Yes. Well, every team in the Southeastern Conference gets five, six million dollars automatically every year.

SC: The Big Ten now has its own television—

CP: Yes.

SC: cable channel.

CP: I once sat with a group of trustees at a Big Ten university that had had a major scandal in intercollegiate athletics. They were talking to me as a potential candidate. I had some interest because I had lots of friends there. One of the trustees said, "Mr. Ping, what would you do to address this problem of intercollegiate athletics we have?" I sarcastically remarked, "The problem is in your hands and solvable overnight. Bo Schembechler and the coach at this campus could just say, 'Our boys are going to have a game on Saturday, and y'all come.' It'd be solved." They didn't think that was funny. [laughs]

SC: [laughs]

CP: But it is, you know. We, as a second-tier conference, are continually struggling to show that we have the same type facilities as the schools that bring in millions and millions. Only a handful of schools in the country actually operate at a profit with their athletic program. But it seems to me if athletics is a defensible educational dimension of a university, then it is desirable for its own sake.

SC: This is primarily for the opportunity that it offers students to participate in athletics as a part of their college life and experience.

CP: Rather than about performance of teams. I think athletics are a primary source of emotive learning. It's the only setting in which great hunks of men can run together and hug each other caught in the excitement of the moment without raising eyebrows. That's important.

SC: What about the notion that athletics is the window on the university? That it's the way of our society, because of the coverage that it receives, that universities have to maintain in order to be known?

CP: Well, I think that's a highly questionable assumption. I think that there's little empirical evidence; there have been some serious studies that it neither contributes to student enrollment, nor giving, except directly to—

SC: athletics.

CP: and I think there is always a core of alumni for whom this is terribly important. I took my lumps on the alumni circuit for team records. I understand this passion for winning. I would certainly rather win than lose.

SC: How do you measure the success of a coach beyond the won-lost record? You were remarkably patient with several football coaches, who seemed to be nice enough men—I liked them in the little interaction I had with them—but both of them had, you know, fairly undistinguished records over a period of time. Was the notion that you got five years, and you understood that, and that then we would have a look? How did you judge them?

CP: Well, if you are going to bring somebody in, you tell them: You have got to see your athletes as young people who are developing, and your concern has to be that they grow academically and personally, not just athletically. You can't simply judge coaches on their won-lost record. You look at the graduation rates. You look at the relationship between the coach and the team, and you give them time. One of the trustees, who was a strong supporter of the administration and who had a very active interest in athletics, said to me when I retired, "Ping, you really were a good president, but you weren't worth a damn picking football coaches." [laughs]

SC: [laughs]

CP: I was serious about asking myself this question. I've seen the other kind of coach too much and understand what they can do.

SC: Football has been much of our subject matter here because it's the one that largely drives the equation nationally, but you were also president at a time when there was a great surge in women's athletics. Some of that was driven by Title IX because somebody had to say it was time. Equal opportunities were offered for women athletes, but I recall your saying, "We're going to do this, and we're going to do this not because of Title IX, but because it's right." And I think that gave everybody a big boost at the time. Do you recall what sorts of battles you had to fight, or arguments you had to use to convince people that it was time that we got square with the women?

CP: Well, one of the great ironies of my life, I was the keynote speaker at the meeting of the National Association of Women's Athletics on the very day that the NCAA made the decision that they would broaden their jurisdiction to include women in sports. I was speaking to this gathering of coaches and athletic directors for women's sports in Houston on the theme: If athletics has a value for the development of men, why doesn't it also have a value for the development of women? I was arguing, of course, that it did. At the end of the session, I had a whole flock of people coming up to me because of the announcement of the NCAA, who were saying, "We're gonna see that we do it differently! We're not going to be—" It didn't turn out that way.

SC: No, it didn't.

CP: I honestly believe that the discipline, the team experience, the whole camaraderie, and the sense that you can become something more that is so basic to serious athletic competition, is usable without reference to gender. So if it's good for the men, it's good for the women. I'm sorry, however, that women's athletics have taken on now million-dollar coaches in basketball, and all the trappings, and all the burdens of intercollegiate athletics in its commercial form. Ohio has not really been subject to the same pressures, but it's still important for a coach to coach a team that wins.

SC: Looking back in terms of the athletic program, is there anything that you didn't do that you wish you had done, or anything you did that you're particularly proud of, besides the issues we circled around?

CP: One thing: Bill Rohr was athletic director, and he had come from Northwestern to Ohio University and really knew the ins and outs of athletics. We had a very blunt conversation as he was about to retire, and he said, "You're naive," to me. He continued, "Unless you're willing to put money on the table, you're not going to get the players you need." He wasn't proposing that we put money on the table, but he was saying that's what it costs. We stayed friends. His wife, Mary Ellen, and Claire are very close, and we stayed close over the years after Bill retired.

A couple of years later Governor Rhodes, as he was prone to do, pulled out of the air an insurance executive named Bill Rohr as a trustee. Of course, there was some "Ah!" Bill and I played golf together from time to time. Just as he was coming on the board, I had a golf round with Bill and said, "It is terribly important, Bill, that you not be seen as a single-issue trustee. You know, you can be concerned about athletics, but don't make that your single issue." He was a balanced, good trustee.

Harold McElhaney was an athletic director who was willing to try to take on what I was trying to accomplish with the NCAA. I hold him in high regard for that. He once told me that one of the things that was decisive in his coming here was that he had read an article that I wrote on intercollegiate athletics. Really, an article written out of a sense of despair and delivered first as an address at a football banquet after a championship season at Central Michigan. He said he had read the article and actually written me a letter. So I went back into my files and, sure enough, there was a letter there. At the time, he was the athletic director at Allegheny College.

SC: What kinds of conversations did you have in your years with your fellow MAC presidents? This must have been something that was a problem for all of you. You've already mentioned that part of it is the trap that we are in. We play at the highest level, but the MAC is not at the highest level in terms of national exposure. So, the dollar returns of playing in this commercial world aren't there. Obviously, you wrestled with it. Did any interesting proposals come up in those years?

CP: Yes.

SC: You can't just unilaterally say you're going to—

CP: Unilateralism in athletics is as unwise as in international relations. I think from time to time there were people within that group who understood that we had a good level of competition, without naive aspirations. I worked well with that group. Sometimes we were fiercely competitive, as with Miami and Bowling Green, for example. Sometimes there were presidents who were willing to take the issue of athletics to the level of the NCAA and fight some of the same battles that I was fighting. But there were also times when I found myself angry and in strong tension with some of the decisions of the conference. I think, probably, the most pointed was when MAC Presidents Council made a decision to go to eighty-five full-ride scholarships for football. I had a very simple study done of the athletes at Ohio University on football scholarships that year. Probably a third, virtually, never made it into a game. So they were supported for four years.

SC: For practice fodder. [laughs]

CP: Yes, well, some as backup—

SC: Right, right.

CP: just in case. Most coaches want some understandable assurance that if they have to, they have someone to turn to. I understand that need, but the truth of the matter is some weren't contributing to the program. However, every one of them was being supported with a full ride. Then the conference was proposing going ten more scholarships in order to stay equal with the big guys. Well, my point of view did not prevail. I also argued that I thought we had a good, sound conference. I had reservations about proposals that the league should expand in some of the directions that were talked about. I had actively opposed the idea that we needed to expand to a size where we could have an east and a west. But we did, eventually, expand. So, yes, I was heartened by the support that some took with them to the NCAA meetings, and at times I was discouraged by the division of athletics in the minds of others.

SC: That raises another issue related to the Mid-American Conference. There's always been a core group of universities that had been members, of which I think we are the oldest, and there have been those who have come in and out, or just in or just out. What issues do you remember, in terms of expansion, when you were president, and how did you feel about it? Was there ever an interest in expanding—you just said you weren't particularly supportive of this east/west, two-division format. Can you talk a little bit about that?

CP: Well, I had a somewhat ambiguous position because I had been provost at Central Michigan University seeking to come into MAC. I was responsible for athletics there and represented the University in all its pleadings with the MAC. In order to accomplish that, there had to be a kind of balance. So two, Central and Eastern, were taken in. Now I found myself saying, "You know, Northern Illinois is a long way away and sort of outside. While Buffalo is a fine educational institution, it's a little bit on our fringe." There were institutions who were proposed for membership that I felt were playing at athletics at a different level with a different set of values.

SC: They shall be nameless.

CP: Yes.

SC: [laughs]

CP: And some were disgraceful. The athletes they accepted were fine athletes and little else and were used to enhance the programs.

SC: Well, if Buffalo was a little too far east, what about Temple and the University of Massachusetts?

CP: Well, that was after my time.

CONVERSATION
with
SAM CROWL

June 2, 2011

SC: Charlie, in our various conversations, we have, of course, talked about people, and we've circled back around some names. I'd like you to take an opportunity now to go through in a more systematic way to talk about key figures in your administration. We'll start once again with the provost and some of the vice presidents, and then we'll move on to the deans. Talk a bit, once again, about the contributions that people like Neil Bucklew, Jim Bruning, and Dave Stewart made to the University as your provosts.

CP: Well, any president who has his wits about him surrounds himself with people who are very able. I was blessed with a whole series of people, and high on the list would be the remarkable provosts that I worked with. The position was defined in my first year, and we began a search. Frankly, I knew from the start who I hoped would emerge from the search, and I would have been bitterly disappointed if he had not, and that was Neil Bucklew. I had worked with him at Central, and I knew that he was an extraordinarily able administrator. He had a bit of the devil in him—

SC: You like people like that.

CP: Yes and—

President Ping with Provost Neil Bucklew, 1981.

Dr. David Stewart, professor
of philosophy and provost,
addressing a class, 1980.

SC: [laughs]

CP: I thought he contributed enormously to the trust with the faculty. I think he had to win it, as we all did, and I think he did. He worked quietly behind the scenes to bring about change, and he was instrumental because he understood much of the structure of planning here. I had designed planning processes on three different campuses, and I learned from my mistakes on the first two. I tried to correct them here. I think Neil had just the temperament as a trained mediator to work with UPAC and other groups with great success, including the Faculty Senate Executive Committee.

SC: Yes. He seemed to be me a man who was most comfortable sitting at a conference table with others hashing out a problem and nothing seemed to ruffle him. He enjoyed the give and take,—

CP: Yes—

SC: which was sometimes a little bitter going back and forth, but he always emerged from it smiling.

CP: Yes, well, he had been in tough labor negotiations, and he knew how to get people to state what they really want, and what they have to have, and then find a way to build conflicting positions into one. We were personal friends and close in many ways.

   A brief personal anecdote—His mother had lived as a widow for many years. My mother died in the early '70s, and my dad lived alone for a number of years. Neil's and our cottages were adjacent to each other in Michigan. So my dad met Neil's mother. Eventually, I'm out playing golf with my father; we were having strained conversations, so I finally said, "Dad, is there something you want to talk about? What is it?" He was asking me for permission to get married. [laughs] I was just overwhelmed by that, and I said, "Dad, anything that helps you live well; I'm in favor."

   Anyway, they were married for the last few years of my father's life. The *Post* got wind of this, and with great indignation published editorials about the deep-seated paternalism and—What's the word?—"nepotism," thank you. So I called the editor over to talk, and I said it never occurred to me to send an invitation to the *Post* when they got married. [laughs]

Anyhow, when Neil left to go to the University of Montana, one of the key people working with him was a longtime faculty member, Jim Bruning. Jim Bruning was a superb provost for many reasons. He had labored long and hard as a member of the faculty, and he understood everything, from the impossible job of a department chairman, to the tensions and conflicts within the faculty. He continued to nurture and to develop the planning process in his own way.

Dr. James Bruning, professor of psychology and provost, pictured here in mid-speech at a dedication of a new computer lab, ca. 1987.

SC: I think the two of you worked together for eleven years,—

CP: Yes.

SC: which is probably a record for a president and a provost.

CP: Yes. I was blessed. We worked well together. There was genuine respect and rapport. In fact, with the whole group of senior officers—Carol Harter turned out to be a great dean of students, and then later as a good vice president for administration. Joel Rudy was instrumental in building character into campus life. He cared so deeply about students. And, Gary North, Gene Peebles, both vice presidents for operations, and the list goes on—

SC: Martha Turnage [vice president for university relations].

CP: Martha Turnage.

SC: I mean, every time I see one of the signs on the side of the buildings, I think of Martha Turnage and the Signage Committee.

CP: Yes, she was instrumental in not just the campus committee but getting signage on the highway that pointed the way

Ohio University Vice President Martha Turnage, influential member of the Signage Committee, 1987.

to the campus. She was an interesting appointment. I made it a practice, when there was a small group of three or so finalists, to go out and meet with them in a private session that was away from the campus, usually near an airport. We would sit and talk for a couple of hours, and I would get some sense if this is a person I could really work with. I had such a conversation with Martha. When I walked her to the gate, for her return flight, we stopped at the gate to say our good-byes, and she turned to me and said, "You haven't asked me about my age." And I said, "Martha, I know how old you are." She said, "I want you to know that I have one more good job left in me." And she did. [laughs] Ah, and there was a whole tier of people that I worked with from Chuck Harrington [director of the Statistical Information Office] to Gary Moden [associate provost] to Chuck Culp, who made the University function. The OHIO campus was blessed by a group of exceptional deans. Each of their names, including yours, should be entered in this account.

SC: Yes. One of the things that impressed me, as I had an insider/outsider relationship with the administration because I had been chairman of the Faculty Senate for a while, and then I became a dean, was that there wasn't a mean-spirited one in the bunch. Usually in any group, there's some-body who has got a chip on their shoulder.—

CP: Yes.

SC: That's the way that they managed their outfits, and it seemed to me, over the years, that those groups took on an aura of being able to get the job done, and they enjoyed—

CP: Yes.

SC: what they were doing. They enjoyed the fact that this was where they were working.

CP: Well, I think that I didn't realize it when I established it, but the 11:30 meetings contributed to that for the vice presidents.

SC: I think, just for the record, we should mention again that Carol Harter went on to become the president of SUNY Geneseo, and on to UNLV. Neil did a stint as the president of Montana, and he returned to his alma mater and did ten years as the president of the University of West Virginia. The longest-standing relationship that you had with any administrator was the one you had with the director of development, who was Jack Ellis, because as far as I know, he spanned your entire career here. He was in place when you—

CP: Yes.

SC: arrived, and he must have retired about the same time, or a little after you did.

CP: Yes.

SC: Talk about that relationship. Once again, Jack was another person who didn't think about it as a job. He seemed to have Ohio University in his system.

CP: Well, more importantly, he was a people person. He cared; he remembered; and he stayed in touch with a very large group of friends of Ohio University.

SC: That's right.

CP: Continuity in development is one of the key elements, and Jack's continued presence here—you know that he worked on two major campaigns —national campaigns. In the first campaign, in the late '70s, there were no computers, and I don't think that we had really used them that much in the second campaign, so Jack was, in many ways, our computer. He was the source of names, and he kept in touch with people, and he genuinely liked talking and talking with them. And he cared deeply about the University. He was our major asset as we began, really, to grow an endowment. We had two very successful national campaigns. At the start of the Third Century Campaign, I remember that we brought in the usual consultant team to help us evaluate how well prepared we were and how much potential we had. They went out and interviewed people all over the country, and they came back and said, "Our best estimate is that you have a potential of about $65 million." That's one of the things these groups are supposed to be able to do. Well, when they shared that with the foundation board, they wouldn't have any part of it. The goal became $100 million. Thanks to Jack Ellis's good work, working with and through a strong core of volunteers, we went well over $100 million.

SC: One of the things that I admired about Jack was the way in which he ran the development office. Whenever the foundation board was on campus, which was two or three times a year, either at one of the luncheons, or at one of the dinner meetings, he always featured a faculty member as the speaker. It seemed to me that was just the appropriate thing to do because it kept faculty in touch with people that they often don't know anything about, who the major benefactors of the University are, and it kept the fund board aware of faculty achievements.

CP: Yes.

SC: Those high-energy faculty members, all the way from the older superstars to the young comers, were there.

CP: Well, it was a very conscious effort on our part. We tried to get to the board some sense of what it was that they were contributing to. I think that friendships developed between board members and faculty members were very strong, but not the kind that go behind the scenes to get something—genuine friendships. That was healthy. It was good. The evidence that it was strong is the number of faculty and staff who were donors to the Third Century Campaign. Eric Wagner, professor of sociology, led the effort.

SC: Let's talk about some of the deans. Obviously, we don't have time to cover every one of the deans, but certainly, one of the ones who made an impact, particularly in using the Stocker gift that you have already talked about, was Dick Robe, who you attracted to campus from Kentucky to be the dean of our College of Engineering.

CP: It took some arm twisting to get him here, although he was a graduate and Athens was his home. Dick and his wife, Ellie, graced the campus. Ellie is the most thoughtful person I've ever met. Dick came into a not altogether happy situation. The faculty had been—

SC: Restive—

CP: Yes, and they were threatened by a lot of things, not the least of which was a sharp decline in enrollment. Dick came in, and he did a superb job in taking this new trust that Paul and Beth Stocker had handed to us. He used it in some very remarkable ways; it became seed money to really grow the future of the college. We did every year, of course, a study of which colleges were a drain on the budget. If you took all the money, all the subsidy, all the tuition, and then you looked at the cost of the college, roughly, which ones were negative.

In those early years, the engineering college was one. By the time I retired, and Dick was at that point retired as well, the college was returning many, many times to the university budget for the college, as a product of external research funding and private support and enrollment. I believe this strongly: Fritz Russ, who was on the Board of Visitors of the college as well as a trustee of the University, monitored very, very closely, year after year, the stewardship of that trust from the Stockers. I think he was impressed with the way Dick used it. Every year, Dick would submit a proposal in terms of how the fund would be used, and every year, I would take a thick notebook describing all that the Stocker money had supported, and then spend the day with Beth Stocker—just keeping her in touch with all that was happening. I think one of the important themes of development is not only the search for support, but also you have to show gratitude and appreciation. It has to be an honest effort to keep—

SC: And to find a way of demonstrating to that external audience what the importance of those funds have been and have meant.

CP: And I think the result of Fritz's assessment—and long conversations that we had about the use of his trust—led to his gift of the Russ Trust, which was a gift of over $98 million from Fritz and Dolores, who did everything together.

SC: Bill Dorrill was the first dean of arts and sciences hired in your administration. We've touched on him briefly when telling the story of the

Mrs. Beth K. Stocker pictured here with three OHIO presidents: (*left to right*) Charles Ping, Vernon Alden, and John Baker. The Stockers' daughter, Jane Norton, stands between Presidents Alden and Baker, 1983.

Chinese intellectuals, and the president [of Peking University] who came to the country in the '70s and made a stop here, as well as at Stanford and Harvard. Talk a little about Bill and his contribution.

CP: Well, he contributed, I think, greatly to the standards for the college by insisting on stricter standards for promotion, which sometimes grated on departments. I think he was also involved in several ways. For example, I think I may have mentioned the fact that he chaired the committee that reviewed my proposal to establish a research foundation. He came back with a counterproposal that we establish an Innovation Center instead.

SC: Bill was also important in the general education movement. He was one of the members of the team who went to Colorado College. He was dogged in seeing that it got passed when it was being debated in the Senate.

CP: Yes. Having the dean of arts and sciences persuaded that this was necessary was very important.

SC: He was, I think, the only one besides Neil and Carol who left the University to pursue a career as president elsewhere. He was the provost at the University of Louisville and then went from there to be the president of Longwood College in the University of Virginia system. Those three presidents—

CP: Yes. Plus Hilda Richards, who was dean of the College of [Health and] Human Services and became chancellor of one of the campuses of Indiana-Purdue.

SC: Bill [Dorrill], who came out of your administration. What do you recall about his successor, Don Ecklemann, who was the dean for the last—

CP: I think he held sometimes too rigidly to standards. He was very hardheaded in most debates, but I think he was important in the development of the College of Arts and Sciences.

SC: Paul Nelson, who was the dean of the College of Communication.

CP: He was a very able dean. The faculty of the College of Communication could, from time to time, be cantankerous.

SC: No.—

CP: [laughs]

SC: Surely you jest.

CP: OK. That's a gentle way of putting it. They were all on Paul's back, from time to time, but I think he led the college well. And, I think, it achieved a steadily growing national recognition. He succeeded John

Wilhelm, who had founded the college and was, in fact, a national figure among war correspondents as well as dean of the college. He was much beloved in that group. Paul was a good and effective dean, and his wife was also an active and well-published member of the faculty.

SC: Judy Pearson.

CP: Judy Pearson. When we had former president Jimmy Carter, the two of them presented a book that they had coauthored—but I talked about that earlier. Paul had a flair and, I thought, was particularly good at speaking to external constituencies.

SC: Yes. He was great talking to alumni or media. He had a spark, and once again, a little bit of the devil in him, as you mentioned about Neil and some of the other administrative colleagues—a twinkle in his eye, which didn't always—

CP: Yes.

SC: serve him well with his own faculty, but I think he was of importance to the University and other constituencies. We've talked about Henry Lin, who was the senior dean when you arrived. Did you understand from the beginning that Henry needed to be treated with a kind of deference that you didn't necessarily have to extend to some of the other deans? He, you know, regarded himself as a figure who was not to be treated lightly.

CP: Did I have a choice?

SC: [laughs]

CP: He was indeed a very remarkable man. He presided over a college that has always been, as is true with most colleges of fine arts, not easy to preside over as a dean.

SC: But as I recall, he also presided over the University Space Committee, and it was almost impossible to get anything done—

CP: [laughs]

SC: or any space rearranged without getting Henry Lin's blessing.

CP: Yes.

SC: I remember conversations with you, in which it was very hard to do long-range space planning, and when that seemed to be the fiefdom—

CP: [laughs]

SC: of one of the deans.

CP: Well, that and the board of regents breathing down our neck about having excess space. I was fond of Henry and have remained close to Julia, his wife, over the years.

SC: Hilda Richards, who was the first dean of the College of Health and Human Services—

CP: Well, Hilda had the perfect academic preparation for being a dean. Her degree was in psychiatric nursing—

SC: [laughs]

CP: [laughs] Hilda, along with Mike Harter, who was a strong associate dean, put the college together. Hilda was a very colorful and dramatic leader for the college. She went on to a provost appointment in Pennsylvania, and Mike should be added to the list of presidents. He now is president of an institution devoted to health professions.

SC: I should have remembered, and Hilda went from there to be head of the Indiana University at Gary [Indiana University Northwest]—

CP: Yes. Yes.

SC: in which you are a kind of mini-president, although they call you a chancellor—

CP: Yes.

SC: so she, too, should be added to our list. Dora Wilson—

CP: Indeed—

SC: who was Henry's successor in the College of Fine Arts.

CP: One of the things that I took some pride in was that we appointed a number of unusual women as the deans and vice presidents, and Dora was one of them. She was a very accomplished artist and a sensitive human being, in an impossible deanship. But part of the place—

SC: Yes, I think at one point, of the seven or eight deans, two were female and also African American, and of the five senior officers, two were female. This was ahead of the national curve in terms of executive appointments.

CP: And they were good appointments.

SC: Yes, exactly. Right. Al Myers in education—

CP: Oh, my, yes. Al also inherited a cantankerous college—most deans do—except for you, Sam, because as the dean of University College, you had no constituent faculty. Al was a long-serving warhorse who knew the ins and outs of colleges. He was an interesting person. He played the

French horn with sufficient skill to be in the university orchestra. He rode bicycles at distances of fifty miles, or more, on weekends. He addressed the key problems of the college.

The College of Education had lost significant enrollment in my early years, because those were the years when teaching was not attracting students. The college had, frankly, an abundance of tenured faculty and a shrinking student population. We tried, Neil and I, consciously to build a staffing model, so that we allowed colleges to reduce their staff over time as retirements created vacancies. We allowed colleges to fill essential positions with the understanding that they had to pay back the position at some future date. Al managed that well. Plus Al, who had had some experience in this area, established very important and very valuable contacts contributing to AID projects in Africa.

Ohio University, going back years before, had had such involvement in Nigeria, and in Kenya. Al encouraged faculty to write proposals that won favor in Botswana, where we had an important role over a fifteen-year period. A large number of our faculty taught for some period of time in Botswana. Our business school faculty in Malaysia, they became faculty at the host institution, and when they came back, they were different because of this experience. Botswana was a project that was well led by Max Evans, and earlier Don Knox.

Years of involvement passed. The project was cited by AID as a remarkable success. It was credited by the government of Botswana as having been an instrumental force in their achieving a national goal of universal primary education. We were there to train the teachers of teachers and to establish a department for this degree program, and we assisted in outreach programs to serve active teachers. On the strength of that success, we won contracts in Swaziland and Lesotho and shared in projects elsewhere.

SC: Talk a bit about the Honors Tutorial College, and Peg Cohn's leadership of it, because it's a unique program in American higher education.

CP: The Honors College is clearly one of the jewels in Ohio University's crown. It was ably led, before Peg, by a mathematician—

Margaret "Peg" Cohn, dean of the Honors Tutorial College, with a student, 1979.

SC: Yes. Ellery Golos.

CP: Peg served with distinction for a number of years as the dean. The Honors College allows bright, self-directed students to build a model on their interests, similar to the tutorial model at Oxford, with a strong relationship with a faculty in an area that they had chosen. That faculty member is their tutor and is responsible for their whole undergraduate program. We've had a steady succession of graduates who have gone on to distinguished careers.

SC: And it turns out, not surprisingly, that those bright, self-directed students, too, need nurturing and nourishing. In many ways, Peg Cohn turned out to be ideal—

CP: Yes.

SC: in that fashion. The students were attached to her, and she was very generous to them with her time—

CP: And she was a well-established scholar with strong research credentials.

SC: Yes.

CP: She was a scientist who was respected by all. She knew how to plan, and how to do research, and I suspect was instrumental in helping many of the honors students learn some of those same skills.

SC: We have talked in previous sessions about the development of the College of Osteopathic Medicine. While Gerald Faverman was the acting dean, it was clearly the case that we were going to have to have a medical person as the dean. So talk about the appointment of Frank Myers, the dean who succeeded Faverman, once the college was up and running.

CP: Well, Gerald Faverman did a magnificent job getting the college off the ground, trampling over people sometimes in the process, but I don't think that we would have managed the tasks without Gerry. He was never the installed dean. Under the rules of the profession, the dean had to be a DO.

   Frank Myers with his quiet, thorough, and careful manner took over the college from Gerry, who had something of a spontaneous and wild manner. Frank worked at building relations with the profession and strengthening the academic program. The college was a work in progress, and we were feeling our way in so many different areas.

   The idea that we would build an internal relationship and use the basic science faculty was a novel experiment, a very successful experiment. The plan to use regional hospitals as teaching sites was also novel. The college is one of, I think, only two medical schools in a small town, or rural area. There simply isn't a population base here to provide the kind of range of experiences students needed. As the medical school grew in numbers, Frank led the way to establish a network of regional teaching sites for their students to—

SC: do their clinical work, yes.

CP: Exactly. And making sure that the standards were consistent was one of the tasks for Frank and the faculty.

SC: He was succeeded by someone with, once again, a remarkable flair. Talk a bit about Barbara Ross-Lee.

CP: Suddenly we had a national figure in the family of the dean of our College of Osteopathic Medicine. Her sister, Diana Ross, an internationally known performer, was here for her installation. Barbara Ross-Lee certainly established a presence in the college.

SC: She came from Michigan State, did she not?

CP: She did.

SC: Where we had a long-standing—

CP: I called the president of Michigan State, who was a friend, and I told him of her candidacy and asked for his counsel. He said, "Well, I think it would be a superb appointment." He turned out to be right.

SC: And, perhaps the first African American woman to head a DO school in the country?

CP: I can't speak with authority, but I think she was. She, in many ways, was in a class by herself.

SC: Yes. Right. Very true.

CP: She was succeeded by a dean who has tirelessly built the school.

SC: And that's Jack Brose.

CP: Yes, a caring, dedicated physician who carried those traits into the planning for the college.

SC: Right. Once again a fine appointment. Let's leave one of the more interesting figures, and one of the more accomplished figures, for last in this list of deans and that's the man who was the dean of the Libraries for most of your time here, Hwa-Wei Lee, who had a lasting impact on the development of the Library into a major and national research institution.

CP: Yes, absolutely. Hwa-Wei Lee served with distinction for a great many years. He retired from the post and in retirement took a leadership role in the Library of Congress.
   Hwa-Wei Lee once said as we sat and talked, "This Library ought to be on the national list of research libraries." I said, "Well, let that be

one of our goals." And, he did. Ohio had added the millionth volume in my first few years here; we added the second millionth volume before I retired.

SC: I think we are at three or more now.

CP: Yes. One of the great issues was how in the world do you build a building to handle a collection when research libraries typically double at about every fifteen to twenty years? Hwa-Wei Lee was in the second half of his career, and he helped solve the problem here.

This wasn't a problem just here. So one of the proposals was space where seldom-used volumes were stored. The Library could use more compact storage space—without room to walk the shelves. Hwa-Wei Lee was instrumental in sorting out the possibilities of an abandoned auto dealership building, and he supervised the conversion. The building itself was finally named for him, and, very gracefully, he presented to the University the two classical Chinese lions that guard the Library Annex. It's a well-designed, useful facility that will serve us for a few years. Then we probably have to replicate it.

Other areas of the state followed a California model involving the building of regional library storage units to serve several universities. But there was no other research university in this part of the state, so we had to do our own.

Hwa-Wei Lee, in achieving the status of a national research library, struggled with the established core of people in the leadership of that institution and their definition of a research library. We were clearly eligible in every standard, except in the number of employees that the Library had. Hwa-Wei Lee was one of the first to see the potential of computer systems in library processes, so we were checking out books using computer systems early.

SC: Yes.

CP: Before other libraries were. Finally he persuaded the association by insisting, "We're adding numbers of volumes, growing the collection; we

A group views the Libraries' one-millionth volume, a thirteenth-century illumi-
nated Bible, given to the University during the 1804 Campaign, 1979.

Marion Alden, wife of President
Vern Alden, uncovers the
Libraries' millionth volume dur-
ing the 175th anniversary of the
University, 1979.

are circulating the number of volumes, and we're using interlibrary loans at a rate—all standards—with fewer staff."

Hwa-Wei Lee also helped cement some of our ties to Asia. He served as consultant to countless universities as China began to open to the world at large. Their universities were growing and trying to become, indeed, contemporary universities. Hwa-Wei Lee was a person who was much in demand to help them in this planning, this development and in training staff. So time after time, I would visit campuses in China, and the librarian would always insist that I visit the library. They would present me with some lovely gift of some Chinese statue, or hanging, or something to express their gratitude to Hwa-Wei Lee and to Ohio University.

SC: One of the measures of our entrance into the exclusive club of research libraries was, I think, that there's something like 120 or 125 of them. When we were finally granted admission, we came in at like 70th, which wasn't as if we were at the tail end.

CP: Yes exactly, that membership was something faculty take particular pride in—

SC: Alden Library—

CP: Everyone who cares about what a university is takes pride in the library.

SC: All right, let's turn the corner now, and talk about some of the faculty that were prominent in your days—and when I say prominent, not only as scholars. We talked about Tom Wagner, John Gaddis, and some others already, who had national reputations. People who were important in the academic community on campus, who were leaders, not necessarily of the Faculty Senate, or politics, just by their presence on campus, and their active involvement in campus issues and academic debates. So, let me start with a wonderful chemical engineer, Nick Dinos.

CP:　Well, let me go back to my first contact with anyone from Ohio University who was a faculty member, Alan Booth, a historian. He was chairman of the search committee. He was a very able teacher, scholar, and authority on Swaziland's history. What caught me right from the start was the depth of his commitment to the institution. He really cared about Ohio. Countless faculty that I met shared that commitment to this institution and its students. Nick Dinos is one. He also is a Renaissance man. He's the only chemical engineer that I ever knew who read philosophy and literature. He was of Greek origin, and we would talk about Kazantzakis, a Greek novelist I admired.

　　When I was confined for six months trying to get my legs to work again, Nick was an attentive friend. Among his gifts to me was a book called *The Philosopher Cat,*—

SC:　[laughs]

CP:　[laughs] and I read it with that kind of glee.

SC:　Someone else who was prominent when you arrived on campus also known as a husband-and-wife team was Hollis Summers and his wife, Laura.

CP:　A wonderful poet whose poetry also had a needle. Only after you sat thinking about the poem, and after you reread it, that it finally penetrated. He and his wife were so gracious, so kind. They went out of their way to make us feel welcome when we came. One of my regrets is that as the years pass there are generations of students who will never know Hollis Summers or Sam Crowl.

SC:　Others will come and take our place.

CP:　Yes. I'm sure. That's a good thing about universities.

SC:　Right. Hollis and Laura lived as you know in a wonderful house at the top of Congress Street that had just an amazing oak tree—

Distinguished Professor of English, influential book collector, and successful author of fiction Jack Matthews, 1976.

CP: [laughs]

SC: in the backyard, and Hollis used to say, "We bought a tree that had a house attached to it."

CP: [laughs]

SC: That house is still in the hands of faculty in the English department: Joe McLaughlin, who was the recent past chair of the department, and his wife, history professor Miriam Shadis, still live there. Jack Matthews was a great colleague of Hollis.

CP: Now if there was ever a man to say the unexpected, it's Jack Matthews. He has a delightful sense of humor, and he is truly a distinguished professor.

SC: Bob Winters.

CP: A fine, fine drama professor who—all these names, they became friends. You're pulling out of my mind all sorts of good memories. Bob, in one of his productions, I've forgotten which one now, demonstrated that while it is hard to get students to do comedy well, it is possible. I don't remember the play, but I remember being so impressed by a comedy that he directed when student actors brought humor. The audience was laughing because it was funny, not because you were supposed to laugh at a particular point. He is a fine theater professor.

I made a conscious effort early on to get to know as many as possible because obviously the faculty, at the time, was angry. The faculty is the heart of the university. They make the university what it is. I was deeply impressed with the loyalty of this faculty. In the two national campaigns that we ran, the percentage of the faculty who participated in the campaign was—I can't cite the number, but it was very remarkable, particularly in the Third Century Campaign. They were generous, generous beyond measure because they were committed to this University.

SC: Once again, that's one of those elements that make us think with some evidence that this is a special place. That sort of devotion goes beyond your professional relationship to the University, to the place itself and a belief in it—

CP: Yes.

SC: and wanting to be a part of it and its success.

CP: I think a great many very able faculty come and stay for many years. Some faculty come, and in their first year, they decide a small town is not for them, and they leave. I didn't understand John Baker's comment to me when he said, "I intended to stay a few years, and I stayed until I retired, and I hope you find that to be true." I did, I'm still here.

SC: Rich Vedder.

CP: A Distinguished Professor of Economics, widely published, a contrarian in most of his approach to research, but he had a breadth of interest that even as he moved to retirement continued to expand to take in new areas. He was a conservative economist, and some of his articles for newspapers ruffled the feathers of legislators.

SC: Well, Rich was one who felt that schools could get along with less money. [laughs]

CP: [laughs]

SC: [laughs] In house we don't need that. We don't need that kind of help with the legislature. But, yes. I just was watching the *MacNeil-Lehrer News Hour* the other night,——

CP: Yes.

SC: and there Rich was on a panel of people talking about the increasing cost of higher education, and whether cost equals value.

CP: This is an illustration of how his interests have been endlessly expanding. He published an important book with the title *Going Broke by Degree: Why College Costs Too Much.* He's leading a national center for the containment of costs in higher education.

SC: Gladys Bailin.

CP: Our dance program—Claire, particularly, took great delight in the program. It has been superb. Gladys Bailin, I think, was also the first woman to be named a Distinguished Professor—

Distinguished
Professor and
director of the
School of Dance
Gladys Bailin, 1986.

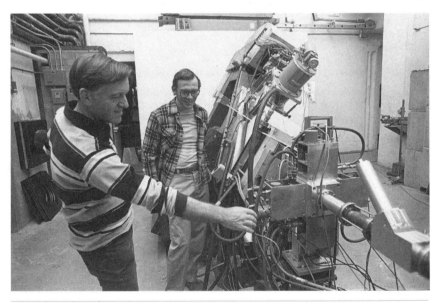

(*From left*) Distinguished Professor Jacobo Rapaport and OHIO's first nuclear physicist, Distinguished Professor Roger Finlay, in the lab with the tandem Van de Graaff accelerator, 1981.

SC: She was.

CP: and she helped create that same quality in the dance program. Her husband who was an artist—

SC: Murray Stern.

CP: was also a very interesting person, and because of my love for athletics, I have one of his drawings hanging in my study to this day.

SC: Roger Finlay.

CP: A very interesting man. A physicist of great reputation, who took a lead role as we were trying to get the third tier of the General Education Program off the ground, and as I remember, he, John Gaddis, and some others—

SC: Dick Bald.

CP: They collaborated on a course dealing with issues related to the nuclear bomb. An intense and again, distinguished scholar, who is rich in his research and the support of his research, an interesting man.

As I was retiring, the Ping Institute for the Teaching of the Humanities was established and endowed. When I came back from my research leave, we got it off the ground. One of the stories that probably most people don't know, which I shared recently at Roger's memorial service: Roger Finlay came to my office one afternoon and said to me, "I've been reading some of the material on this new Institute for the Teaching of the Humanities, and I understand that there are to be two in-house faculty positions created as faculty of the institute. Would it be possible to consider a physicist? I'm at a turning point. Either I continue in ever deeper dimensions to pursue my research at Los Alamos"—he had an appointment out there for leave—"or I turn in some different directions. And I think I'm interested in some of the things you're describing."

Professor Richard Bald, instrumental in getting the University's General Studies Program off the ground, pictured here in 1981.

SC: I had not known that.

CP: I said, "Roger, that would be exciting, but we are limited to the National Endowment's definition of the humanities, and I don't think it includes physics, I'm sorry to say."

SC: Betty Hollow—

CP: is a sensitive person. In the bicentennial year, she wrote a superb history of the institution drawing heavily on the archives. There are all sorts of wonders in those archives, the history of students and the history of the campus.

SC: The social history of the University—more than it is an academic history—

CP: Yes. So many of the histories that have been published have followed the succession of presidents as the outline.

SC: Right. And she gets at the history from the bottom up.

CP: Yes.

SC: Remarkable. Butch [Herman W.] Hill—

CP: Butch is my successor with a program that I love, and I hope that we talk about at some point—the Cutler Scholars Program. Butch is an electrical engineer who—I think Nick Dinos is his role model—like Nick has a breadth of interests and concerns. I have watched Butch lead the colloquia sessions of the Cutler Scholars Program for years now. In the fall, we deal with a topic in government and politics, and Butch identifies the topics and then leads the Cutler colloquia. In the winter, we deal with something more in his line of science and technology, and then in the spring, we follow the Baker Peace Conference topic. And this means that he's dealing with a range of subjects with two groups of students every week. What a remarkable mind, and what a breadth of interests, and what a genuine deep interest in and concern for students.

SC: Steve Hays.

CP: Bless his heart. He sometimes appears on campus looking like the *American Gothic*—

SC: [laughs]

CP: when he appears in his overalls. He is a man who loves his discipline, and who transmits his love of Classics to his students. We had the largest enrollment in Classical Greek on any campus in the country in at least one year, maybe more than one year, and he was justly proud of it. Why did we have it? Because Steve went out and hustled the students. He told

Attendees crowd the Templeton-Blackburn Memorial Auditorium for the Baker Peace Conference, 1990.

them all the wonderful things that came with the Classics, and how rewarding it is, and how much it can mean for their future. He has continued to try to mine that sort of general educational commitment. When the Faculty Senate just seems to not be able to come to grips with it, Steve and Tom Carpenter, and others, have come together and have done something important in general education within the College of Arts and Sciences. A wonderful effort.

SC: Someday someone ought to write a sort of brief history of the department of Classics, now Classics and World Religion, because it ran against the wave.

CP: Yes, and George Weckman is an important part of that story and history, as is Tom Carpenter.

SC: When I got here there were one and a half members of the Classics department. It was clearly dying, and nobody cared very much. Nationally the Classics were dying, and accounting was getting new professors—dollars following students. I think Steve was hired, mainly, because we would be embarrassed if we couldn't offer beginning Latin and Greek. Paul Murphy had retired. And in three or four years, as you say, Steve had built the beginning Greek and Latin classes and was allowed to hire another faculty member. Now there are about ten members of the department.

CP: Yes.

SC: So I think it is just a remarkable story.—

CP: Yes it is.

SC: He was the fire that got it going.

CP: And, a constant burr under the administration's saddle. That's healthy. He is really committed to the institution and its students.

SC: As long as you've just mentioned him, why don't we talk about Tom Carpenter, who is the Ping Professor of Humanities, a major faculty member, and former chair of the Department of Classics and World Religions.

CP: Well, to set the stage, I have to talk about something that really belongs to my retirement years, and that's—

SC: Well, shall we save it?—

CP: No. An institute. An Institute for the Teaching of the Humanities that was a product of a proposal, Sam, that you and Dave Stewart prepared for the National Endowment of the Humanities. To our delight it was funded, I think, to the level of $300,000 on the condition that it would be matched three-to-one. The proposed institute was to be dedicated, not to research, but to teaching in the humanities.

There are lots of research institutes, but this was to be a special institute. The proposal said that the institute would try to nurture the sense of community within the humanities faculty and strengthen their role in general education. It would reach out to public schools and try to build within the teachers of humanities at all levels in the state a sense of a common celebration of the humanities. There were to be two faculty in-house, and the endowment was to bring to campus a new faculty member whose salary would be divided between the endowment and the general fund.

Once we had the grant, we weren't having much success in getting the money matched. I don't know who thought of the idea, but I'm deeply grateful. As I was nearing retirement, someone put the idea forth that it might be created—and I didn't know about this—in my name. A group of trustees of the foundation and the University immediately enlisted in the giving and getting of funding. The condition of the receipt of the grant money from the national institute was that the $300,000 had to be matched at least three-to-one, and we ended up matching by far more than three times the grant.

All of this was done without my knowledge. When it came before the board of trustees, it brought tears to my eyes because teaching and the teaching of the humanities has been at the center of my life.

Anyway, I am sorry that I got off on the side. Once we got the two in-house faculty appointed, and the original grant writers involved, we were beginning to form a group of faculty and fellows—we launched a national search for the new appointment. That was probably the most exciting faculty search that I had ever been part of because we advertised insisting that this person had to have an established reputation in teaching. The individual had to be recognized for outstanding teaching, *and* had to be a nationally and internationally known scholar—an active, contributing scholar.

It was such a delight. We had a whole pile of nominations. After reading them, they restored your faith in the fact that you could have a campus with a core of faculty who were researchers, and who were dedicated to teaching. We brought three to campus for interviews, and any one of whom would have been great—it was just breathtaking. Tom Carpenter was the person that we chose—what a happy and wonderful choice. He is a Classics professor, an international authority of the images of Dionysus, well published, an Oxford PhD, and he and his wife, Lynne Lancaster, who is an equally accomplished scholar—

SC: Also an Oxford PhD—

CP: have graced our faculty ever since. He has been a presence, pushing for what I talked about with Steve Hays, the effort to salvage a floundering discussion of general education.

SC: And has actually created a program in Arts and Sciences that is an attempt to make an integrated approach in the freshman year to general education distribution requirements.

CP: I think that he has chaired and led the Ping Institute in a remarkably effective manner.

SC: Guido Stempel. We haven't talked about a journalist.

CP: Well, he is a Distinguished Professor of Journalism who again was widely published, mostly in print media. He also is an outstanding teacher with a nice touch for irony that continues even into retirement.

SC: Duane Schneider.

CP: Duane Schneider was a recognized scholar with an interest in Dickens—

SC: Oh, well, lots of people, Anaïs Nin was the subject of his book. Charles Dickens was his favorite author to teach.

CP: He gave some very interesting lectures on Dickens. He took on the Ohio University Press and provided, I think, leadership that saved the press at a time that it was in jeopardy. He led the way for the combining of the Ohio University Press and the Swallow Press. I remember presenting it as a recommendation to the trustees.

Kenner Bush, third generation of his family to be a trustee, and a superb trustee, spoke with me as we took a break. He said, "Charlie, let me understand this. I'm going to support you, and what you're recommending, but we've got a problem. We've got a press that's losing money, and you want to buy another press that's losing money. We'll combine these two losers, and then we'll have a money maker? You know that I'm the editor and publisher of a newspaper—that's a little hard for me to swallow, but I'll support you in this." [laughs]

SC: Kenner was right. [laughs]

CP: [laughs]

SC: Let's turn and talk about what you did to, at least momentarily, get the University out of your system. I know Claire was important in this and that she would arrange maybe every couple of months to find a weekend when you could get away from—

CP: Yes.

SC: the fishbowl of the campus. What ways did you find to refresh yourself, even when you couldn't get away for any length of time?

CP: There are two things about a presidency that make it a strain: One, you can't have really close friends—sometimes there are other presidents, but everybody's busy. The second thing is that you can't get away from it, particularly if you live in a presidential residence on campus.

Faculty come to campus; they teach their classes and do research, and then they go home. Well, I work all day and go home, and I'm still on the campus. That invites students, unannounced and uninvited, to knock on your door. It invites an endless sound—and it invited pickets in the one strike that we had. It means that you are on call in some surprising ways, twenty-four hours a day, seven days a week.

I remember an absolutely frantic graduate student who had left the Library to get something to eat. He came back only to find the Library closed and all locked up, and his dissertation, which at the moment he was finishing, was locked up in the Library. There was no one there to let him in. He asked me if I could *please* let him in or find someone—

Well, one of the things that I insisted on was that I have a key to every building on campus. I'd learned that lesson on another campus. So I took him over to the Library, and we went and got the material that he needed, and he managed to survive and meet his deadline. But you know, this is two o'clock in the morning or something.

Anyway, Claire was very sensitive to the fact that there were times when you just find this a strain. She would call Marie White and say, "All right, next weekend is to be clear." She loved to travel by the back roads and book country inns. I was less enthusiastic, as most of the beds in the inns were too short, but we would have a trip, and she would plan it. We went to some interesting places. That's how I first found out about New Harmony, Indiana, an historically important community in southern Indiana established by a sect committed to an ideal. We saw lots of Shaker communities. Anyway, it was a way that we would be together and get away.

The president's house is used heavily as a place to entertain on-campus groups of faculty and students as well as a great many guests of the University. Claire entertained over fifty thousand people in the almost two decades that we lived at 29 Park Place. We had to be able to report numbers and names to the Internal Revenue Service.

SC: Talk a little bit more about her role, and how she saw the two of you as a partnership in this endeavor.

CP: I don't know that it was a conscious or a deliberate decision or something that we even talked about, but she stepped in and took charge. My first need was to get close to the faculty, so we began to have afternoon teas for University Professors and Distinguished Professors. The teas were mostly just talk; I'd ask them about their interests to get a feel for it. Claire enjoyed this as much as I did. We also had groups of students in. She was always the first person at the door to greet them. She was the one who took the time to memorize guest lists; she was also the one who closely monitored what was served in the president's house. She was responsible for menus, planning, and the presentations.

We didn't have any money. I mean that the University didn't have any money, but thanks to our predecessor, and particularly his wife, who had done a magnificent job in refurbishing the furniture in the house and redecorating, we were able to build on what they had done. We essentially used the first floor of the house as public space. For example, on Moms Weekend, we'd hold a coffee and muffins reception for all the mothers on campus. We would have six hundred or seven hundred mothers come through the house. We had students who led them on a tour of the house. We discovered, only after some time passed, to our surprise, that drawers that were really personal were regularly opened and explored.

SC: [laughs]

CP: In ways that you wouldn't believe. [laughs] Well, I think she genuinely enjoys people and began to get to know many influential women, because we entertained a lot of townspeople. She formed a circle of women with whom she was very close: Ann Grover, Marion Lavelle, Verda Jones, Jean Sprague, to name just a few.

SC: Margene Bush. Osie T. Collins, was she a part of that—

CP: Yes. And Faye Klahn.

SC: Right.

Claire Ping speaks with Musa Hitam, deputy prime minister of Malaysia, and the Malaysian minister of education, Tun Abdullah bin Haji Ahmad Badawi (the future prime minister), ca. 1980s.

CP: Anyway, together they helped preserve the downtown of Athens, and they organized the Athens Foundation. They were an active downtown preservation group. They were a constant presence.

Our entertainment at the president's home created some problems. I'm such a sore loser that when we had after-game meals for athletic supporters and others, frankly, I was barely civil to people after a trouncing. So one day Claire said, "You know, I don't think this is a good idea. I think we ought to do pregame brunches; at least you'd have the hope." [laughs] And we did. [laughs]

SC: [laughs]

Formal portrait of Ohio
University President
Charles Ping and his wife,
Claire, on their tenth an-
niversary as president and
first lady.

CP: We switched from after-game to pregame. One of the amusing inci-
dents at a dinner after a game: The house was full of people and all sorts
of delightful conversations, when an unexpected and uninvited guest, a
very large man, showed up at the door. He was well into his cups; in
short, he was very drunk. [laughs] He was there to protest the fact that
the football coach was not using his son as much as he thought that he
ought to be used. He came through the door and started backing me
down the hall, when one of our alumni, who was about half his size,
suddenly took it upon himself—an alumnus from Boston whom you
know well—to defend me against this [laughs] aggressive, large man,
whose son, I suspect, was a lineman. Eventually, the two of us managed
to maneuver our uninvited guest out the door.

There are many, many experiences. I think having those groups in
and having a chance to talk to people contributed to a strong base of
support from people like Ed Kennedy and others, who appreciated and

understood the importance. Our children suffered through this. Our son was a senior in high school and our daughter a high school freshman when we came. I explained to the trustees that there was one condition I insisted on: Friday nights are reserved, and I went—

SC: To the Friday night high school football games.

CP: to the football games and the basketball games. Sundays were largely reserved also. Our daughter simply retreated from most of this. By the time our grandsons were old enough to be a part of the scene, they enjoyed it.—

SC: They loved it.

CP: Yes. They [laughs]—

SC: [laughs]

CP: I looked around, and here was my ten-year-old grandson, Sam, serving cocktails to guests—oops [laughs]—

SC: [laughs]—

CP: Claire was my rock—everyone needs someone. When you've gone through a day in which everyone in one way or another was coming in and saying, "You S.O.B., blah, blah, blah, " and you go home and there is someone who will accept you and say, "Well, maybe you're not so bad," that makes the next day possible.

SC: I know besides those short little getaway weekends, both of you share a love for England, for London, in particular, and the theater. Do you know where that came from in your past? I mean, how did the two of you discover that was a mutual pleasure?

CP: Claire's maiden name was Oates, and that's a very English name. Well, she loves preservation. She loves the villages and the gardens. When you compare the French gardens and the English gardens, the British have a wonderful sense of—it's planned, but it's not planned.

SC: Right. It's on a human scale—

CP: Yes. And I was an English literature major as an undergraduate.

You and Susan were so kind to Claire and me, and we shared the experiences with Will and Ann Lee Konneker; in a modest way, we had your love of London. And you helped us to see London through your eyes; you helped plan a number of wonderful weeks when we would come to London. Every night, sometimes matinées in the afternoon, we'd go to a play. You would carefully select the plays. It would be everything from Shakespeare to contemporary musicals. We cherish the memories.

Obviously, we went to Stratford, and we saw Shakespeare plays and got to meet directors through your good offices. You and Susan loved the British Library. We have learned to share that love and to delight in the British Museum in London. I remember cab rides—I even remember your taking us to a pub the London cab driver couldn't find, and you had to direct him.

Will and Ann Lee Konneker and Claire and I traveled together to many points around the globe.

SC: Malaysia—

CP: Botswana, Namibia, South Africa. Most of the trips to Asia were on University business. But southern Africa was sheer pleasure.

SC: Asia.

CP: Particularly to Asia. Will and Ann Lee even went with us to Taiwan when I was receiving an honorary degree. We loved traveling and sharing with them. But the highlights were our trips to London and our theater experiences.

SC: Well, they were for us, too.

CP: To get that sort of break from routine. It re-energized us. That's not the pattern of many presidents.

SC: I agree. I mean, not every president thinks, "Gee, a week in London, the British Museum, and the theater every night, that's what relights my fire and gets me going again." But, I'm pleased that was your relaxation.

CP: And I'm pleased that we could share London with you and Susan.

AC: Let's do one last little number about people, and these are a different sort of people. These were the major visitors who came to campus. We talked about Jimmy Carter a great deal, so we know about him. But who were some of your favorites of the many writers and diplomats, politicians, and scholars who have—

CP: Well, interestingly enough, Alex Haley was one of my favorites, Haley the author of *Roots: The Saga of an American Family*. He was on campus just as *Roots* was creating a national interest. We had a dinner party for him, as we tried to do for all the Kennedy lecturers. He was seated next to Claire at one end of the table engaged in conversation, and they began to talk about Tennessee—her home is Tennessee, west Tennessee—and if you remember the *Roots* story, it ends up in Henning, Tennessee. Well, Henning is very near Kerrville, Claire's home. The two were reveling in their shared sense of Tennessee. I watched that from the other end of the table with delight.

Alex and I had time to talk when a television series was made of his book. I had read the book a couple of times. He was a remarkable man.

SC: You corresponded with him for a time—

CP: Yes, I did. For a number of years. He had limited education; he had been in the Coast Guard. His first writing experience was for fellow servicemen who asked him to write their love letters home to girlfriends. He made the letter a little grander than they could. [laughs]

SC: [laughs]

CP: Of course, his collaboration with Malcolm X was an important part of his career.

SC: Who else?

CP: Well, let's see. My least favorite—

SC: Yes, I know. Go ahead, go ahead [laughs]

CP: [laughs]

SC: with your least favorite.

CP: Well, it was a man who revolutionized television news reporting. Ted Turner. We had a dinner for him and other guests. Claire had put a white chocolate mousse dessert on the menu. I couldn't help but overhear him, though I was at the other end of the table, and Ted Turner ate the dessert, and he turned to Claire and said, "Ma'am, that was just fine puddin'."

He went on to deliver a lecture after which—I was very proud of our students—he obviously was playing to the audience and pampering them in irritating ways. They didn't fall for this at all. Once the question period began, they asked him questions that subtly and, I thought, wonderfully, exposed all the pretense of his lecture. I think that's the reason I enjoyed his lecture.

Well, I think I said that former President Carter is high on that list because he took such care to be in a particular place and a particular campus,—

SC: Yes.

CP: and we had psychologists and botanists, and we had literary figures—
        it was an endless stream. Someone asked, "What do you miss the most
        about the presidency?" I think I miss the opportunity to meet such peo-
        ple and talk with them.

SC: Let's turn and do one more. When you're talking about the meeting
        and the greeting and the way of having a personal impact on people, you
        were talking in terms of visitors to the house. What were some of the
        ways that you tried to do this with the more far-flung alumni world?
        How did you try to reestablish alumni ties? One of the crises you came
        into was an alumni disaffection to the place, and one of the things that
        we know about our alumni is they love this place. They have great fond
        memories of it, but given the times, and the fact that they were seeing the
        University in the newspaper in not always flattering lights, what steps did
        you try to take to heal that breach?

CP: Well, I think that is a description of the attitude. One of our distin-
        guished alumni was a prominent editor in New York City. As I was com-
        ing into office, he gave me a large notebook which he had titled, "The
        Good, the Bad, and the Ugly." He had clips from the *Plain Dealer* and
        from newspapers all over the country. News reports that reflected very
        badly on his alma mater, and he said to me in very direct terms, "I want
        this changed."
            We needed the support of the alumni. We needed it in student re-
        cruitment. We needed it if we were going to have any successful develop-
        ment effort. So, with Claire at my side, I very consciously invested a lot
        of time in strengthening alumni relations, and in some cases with strong
        alumni directors and the board, helping established alumni groups all
        over the country and overseas as well. As I said earlier, we made a regular
        Florida run and met with three or four alumni groups, out of which
        we drew very loyal supporters and very active contributors with Leona

[Hughes] leading the list. But, also, in major cities around the country: Chicago, New York, Boston, and San Francisco.

You were at one of the events in Boston. We were the first outside group to be allowed to use the Kennedy Library. Led by Bob Axline and Sandy Elsass, we held the Boston area alumni meeting during the 175th anniversary year. You played Manasseh Cutler in a historical sketch. We served the Massachusetts Alumni Chapter a meal similar to one Manasseh Cutler had been served in the White House by Thomas Jefferson. That was just a very special alumni event and year.

SC: Right.

CP: In San Francisco, San Diego, Los Angeles and Phoenix, and Atlanta and on and on and on, we tried to identify potential leadership, and we went out. Frankly, to continue the story, I remember early on that I kept getting beat up about: "What are you going to do about this party school image?" I got so sick and tired of hearing that that I finally developed a response.

I got the figures on the number of people who came into Alden Library on a daily count, the number of books circulated, and the number of requests for interlibrary loans. So I would respond, "They do like to have a good time, and they are noisy at times, but let's look at the broader picture. Do you know they take"—I don't remember the number—"150,000 books out of the Library every week. If so, somebody's doing something else other than partying. If they are, in fact, requesting thousands of interlibrary loans, you know, I'm sorry, but there is another side." And then I went on to talk about the faculty, students, and some of the things that were important to campus life.

SC: Did you consciously devote a certain percentage of time—10, 15, 20 percent—to those visits, to going out to alumni chapters? Did you have a calculus in mind?—

CP: No, I didn't. I tried to combine the meetings with other business and with fund-raising. If I was going to the west coast to speak at some meeting, I would arrange a visit to San Francisco, or Los Angeles and San Diego, or Phoenix, or something as part of the trip. If I was going to be in Denver for some meeting—

But I thought it was very important, particularly in the early years. Once I had done it, I [laughs] got on the circuit. I think that the alumni meetings were an investment. If you look at the figures for the number of alumni who contributed in our first national campaign—the 1804 Campaign—then you look at the jump in the number of alumni who contributed in the Third Century Campaign, you see why it was so important to devote that time. Now, much of alumni giving was modest, but this is the base that you build on.

SC: One of the things that I had tried to sell to a previous administration and had gotten nowhere, you picked up on immediately. That was the idea of starting an Alumni College to bring alumni back to campus to be able to see the quality of the faculty in action here. That was another program that helped to repair whatever fissures there were between the University——

CP: It was an idea that you brought to me, and I welcomed it. Universities relate to their alumni, it seems to me, every way, except what they are about as universities—or too many of them do. They have events surrounding away football games, but I got pretty tired of them, and they have events surrounding athletic events of other sorts, but they very seldom relate to the business of intellectual exploration—

SC: Right.

CP: the excitement—

SC: Sharing ideas.

CP: Sharing ideas. We have a wonderful faculty, and with your help, we enlisted the very best of our faculty to spend an hour with the Alumni College—it might be a scientist, it might be a historian—with a core group of alumni who got so caught up in that that they came back every year. It was, I think, a great success.

Alumni are important for another reason. When you go to foundations, one of the first questions you get asked is, "What level of support do you have from alumni?" Our alumni support was very persuasive. Let me talk about another subject—

SC: OK. Sure.

CP: if we have a moment. This University has been blessed with a set of trustees genuinely interested in and willing to give time to the distinctive quality of academic life of Ohio University. By statute, a majority of Ohio trustees must be graduates. We have had, and I've been close to trustee appointments continuing even to the present, a remarkably dedicated group of trustees. We've had some people who were willing to spend time bringing the University along in its development and helping. People like Fritz Russ in engineering, Jenny Grasselli in the natural sciences—

SC: Bob Axline in business.

CP: Bob Axline was never a trustee, but you're right—

SC: Well, true, sorry.

CP: a foundation trustee and that's another whole story.

SC: Right.

CP: Ed Kennedy was on the board when I came, and he was another of the reasons that I came to Ohio University. I quickly caught a sense of their genuine commitment. It was a diverse group with a diverse set of interests. But I count Ralph Schey among my mentors, and I count Kenner Bush, who was a very dedicated and good trustee, a mentor for me. Good in the sense that he was not only involved here, he took time

Trustee Donald Spencer (*left*) and his wife, Marian, 1983.

to be involved in Columbus on behalf of the University. Dean Jeffers, who was a leading corporate executive and understood the role of the board, not all trustees on all campuses do. But I think people like Dean and Ralph helped the board. Ralph Schey was a source of constant encouragement and enlightenment for me. You know the love of the place by people like Milt Taylor and Jody Phillips was contagious.

SC: Even people who never went to school here—I'm thinking of Don Spencer, who became very attached—

CP: who adopted the place—

SC: Right.

CP: Yes, and he established a student award that he granted every year. Yes, and Charlotte Eufinger, another classic case. They're very special people. I became close friends with many of them, and it wasn't a formal relationship, but it was, I think, a relationship that enriched my life, encouraged me, and sustained me throughout. They attracted me here, and I think one of the reasons that I stayed nineteen years was the board of trustees. They had the good judgment, which is not altogether common on boards, from time to time to recognize the need for professional development.

You know, day in and day out being a university president can be very draining and demanding. The board was kind enough to grant me sabbaticals. Not full sabbaticals, but generous sabbaticals of a few months. So once I went off to Harvard, and I was a visiting professor for three months. Another time I went off to Manchester in England and taught as a visiting professor.

I remember coming back from the Harvard stint, and at my first Faculty Senate meeting someone said, "Well, President Ping, you've just come back from being a faculty member at Harvard on a leave. How'd you like it?" I said, "You know, I would spend my days in a comfortable office on campus, occasionally meeting with students. I taught a seminar, and I had time to do some serious research. Every night I was privileged, in twilight, to walk across the Harvard campus to the condo where we were staying. In the twilight, I would think to myself, 'You know, there are people getting paid to do this.'" [laughs] I don't think the Faculty Senate thought that was funny.

SC: [laughs] Oh, they knew what you were talking about.

CP: [laughs] But the board in its wisdom gave me those opportunities. I came back refreshed. Frequently with ideas, new directions, and enthusiasm that I don't think I would have had without—

SC: Great.

CP: Every summer I was off a week to teach at Harvard. Anyway, it was a board that was supportive and understanding, but I always tried to be a good steward of their trust.

CONVERSATION
with
DOUG McCABE

June 7, 2011

DM: I am Doug McCabe, curator of manuscripts and the producer of this video. I am filling in for Sam Crowl today. I thought we'd start this interview today by discussing your personal philosophy and how that was put to use in your career and your personal life.

CP: Well, I have taught philosophy on several campuses as well as here. So after I left office, I did something useful: I taught philosophy. My particular area of interest is nineteenth-century German philosophy, but more broadly, my interest is the history of philosophy.

I am deeply influenced by the idealistic tradition that stretches back to Plato and spent several years of my life translating Hegel, a nineteenth-century idealist. Out of that work, I gained a sense of how useful ideals can be. They may never be realized, but I start with a vision of what it ought to be and try to make the world or its institutions as nearly like the ideal as possible.

From this study of Hegel, I became caught up in "wholeness" themes. If you have ever read Hegel's *Philosophy of History,* for example, you know that he undertakes to build a sense of a connected whole that unfolds. Out of this wholeness comes an insistence that the whole defines the part and that the whole is a set of interconnected parts. That is a philosophical theme, which is reflected in most of the things I talked about and did.

"Wholeness" and "ideals" were very much a part of my professional life as president.

DM: What got you interested in philosophy in the first place?

CP: I came into college completely innocent of any knowledge of philosophy. In my freshman year, I had a wonderful multidisciplinary course. One of the early assignments in this course was to read the Socratic dialogue of Plato, *The Apology*. Since then, Socrates has been a constant companion. I come back to the three Socratic dialogues and reread them over and over and over.

When each of my grandchildren graduated from high school, I presented them with three books. Each one was inscribed. One was a marvelous edition, an annotated translation with Sir Richard Livingstone doing the notes, of the three Socratic dialogues. The book is long out of print; I searched, found copies, and inscribed them as one of the three books. A copy of a dictionary was the second, a good dictionary; because I think the use of language is the mark of an educated man. Finally, because faith is very important to me, a particular translation and study edition of the Bible: Those were the three books that went to each one of my grandchildren.

DM: Well, let's hope that they appreciated all three. [laughs] I would guess that it's rather unusual for grandchildren to receive something like that, but maybe it is not a surprise coming from you. how does this ideal within philosophy apply? Specifically, how does it apply as a university administrator, as a provost, as a president?

CP: Well, I sought to help institutions to understand what they should be and then work to approximate that ideal.

DM: So, here we are with the wholeness idea. Apply that to athletics—

CP: Yes.

DM: Or a departmental philosophy, or the history department, or biological studies, and so forth.

CP: Well, if you go back to my annual convocation addresses, you will find that theme over and over and over again. How does it apply to each of those? I think, in my vision of what a university ought to be, athletics has a place on campus because they are an integral part of the educational activity. They teach the wonder of emotive learning, and, I think, a great many other lessons. I regret the character of contemporary athletics, but I think athletics on campus have a role, just as I think the philosophy department has a role.

Eighteenth president of Ohio University, Dr. Charles Ping (1975–94).

I think the philosophy department teaches various topical subsets: epistemology, linguistics, and ethics; it teaches a whole set of different things. But for me, the heart of what a philosophy department does is tied to the history of philosophy. I taught philosophy, even when I was sitting in the president's office, from time to time. If all you read closely are the things that come across a president's desk, you would dry up and blow away.

DM: [laughs]

CP:　But reading Kierkegaard, Nietzsche, Hegel, and a whole set of nineteenth-century figures enriched life.

Well, for the same reason intercollegiate athletics can be important in the lives of young people, I think some of the same values come from intramural teams. As a faculty member, I remember for years competing on intramural basketball and volleyball teams. I was much younger then.

DM:　[laughs] Your knees were in better shape.

CP:　Yes. That's true.

DM:　The other thing, too, about intramurals is that here's an opportunity for students in particular to participate—

CP:　Yes.

DM:　in an active way as opposed to being observers or fans.

CP:　There are different skill levels. There are varsity sports, club sports, and intramural sports, and each tries to give as broad an opportunity as possible. That's the ideal.

DM:　Right. There you go.

CP:　[laughs]

DM:　Not everybody participates, but those who do, I think, enjoy it immensely—even broomball. [laughs]

CP:　Yes, indeed. I think there's also a range of activities that enlist the participation. One thing, I know, is at the start of exam week there is a dodge ball competition going on. How sensible is it to pick up a ball and throw it at somebody during exam week—it is probably a therapeutic thing.

DM: [laughs] Another area of wholeness and broadening would be student activities in the form of fraternities, sororities, and then all of the club-type activities, which could be anything from swimming, to horseback riding, to also, well, debate—

CP: Yes.

DM: and lots of other areas that are available to students.

CP: Again, wholeness is an equestrian team, a debate team—some of the same values are being exercised by their participation.

DM: And by being outside of class and requiring activity.

CP: Yes.

DM: I think another thing I was so impressed with when I returned to the University was the General Education Program. By the time I came back, I was essentially in my senior year. So it was, for me, taking a Tier III course with the idea that I understood the ideas behind it, which was to bring together a lot of the things that one was picking up in various disciplinary areas—

CP: Yes.

DM: and combining them into something meaningful. I really enjoyed taking the Tier III course that I took.

CP: Well, the concept of Tier III came out of the work of the general education committee. It represents an effort to teach students to think in these ways; it was an effort on the part of faculty to design courses together. So it was of as much value for the faculty as it was for the students.

Earlier I pointed to a physicist and a historian and others who were involved in a Tier III course in nuclear deterrent and threat—

DM: I took that very course.

CP: Oh, did you.

DM: Yes.

CP: Well, you had John Gaddis, and you had a physicist—

DM: Roger Finlay.

CP: Roger Finlay and—

DM: And Dick Bald.

CP: and Dick Bald. The fact was that they had talked to each and worked to put this together—

DM: My only complaint was that we had to take three midterms and three finals; in essence, I had to take an exam from each of them. That was a lot of work, but at the time, I was of an age that I didn't mind it. I enjoyed the course so much—

CP: Yes.

DM: because of that melding of the disciplines and bringing that all together. I think that really speaks well, not just for general education, but also in the broader sense, to that idea of wholeness and—

CP: Yes.

DM: that idea of a liberal education and what that really means.

CP: Yes, and that was very consciously a part of the design, an ideal.

DM: I remember thinking, too, how I felt sorry for students at other places who might not have been asked, or required, to do those kinds of courses. Specifically, not only in a discipline they're majoring in, but also in the broader sense for life skills. Those courses can be more than just how to raise a family, but how—

CP: Yes.

DM: how to think.

CP: Yes, indeed.

DM: So, there we are with philosophy. Now maybe we can move on to what some people might call a branch of philosophy, I suppose, but in other ways, it's something very different, and that is religion. You are, and have been for many, many years, an ordained minister. I also think that an ordained minister as president of a public university is highly unusual. It was not two hundred years ago, as we both know, Ohio University was under the control of your very Presbyterians—

CP: Yes.

DM: for a number of years, before those rotten Methodists wrestled away—

CP: [laughs]

DM: the presidency.

CP: In fact, the first four presidents were Presbyterian clergymen and served the local church as well as the University. That was not uncommon in that day. I think it was only in the late nineteenth century that you began to get a more careful reading of the concept of the constitutional separation of church and state. My wife and I were married right

President Ping in a collegial conversation on the steps of the historic Cutler Hall, 1979.

after graduation. We went from a college to a seminary. My first graduate degree was in theology. At the time, my thought was that I would become a pastor. However, I got increasingly interested in serious intellectual research and won a doctoral fellowship, and off we went.

My career was in teaching. I taught the history of philosophy. I also taught, frequently, the philosophy of religion, and I didn't find personal conflict in that. My career was entirely in the private sector up to the time I agreed to come to Central Michigan as provost. I had a great deal to learn about the public sector, and I very consciously tried to honor the separation of church and state.

We are a public university, and we have a public mission. I'm sure the trustees knew because I certainly have not ever kept it a secret—that my faith is who I am.

For example, I said to the trustees, "I'm not going to schedule things, unless it is absolutely necessary, on Sunday, or for that matter, on Friday night, because of high school athletics and my children; Sunday because that was personal time." Consciously, during my years as president, I was not active at the various governance levels of the denomination. I said to them, "If you meet on Sunday that would be fine." Typically, since the delegates to the several courts are pastors and elders in the Presbyterian tradition, they meet during the week. I had other obligations during the week.

I remember a question that was asked Jimmy Carter that I thought was an exceptionally good question. A student asked him, "Mr. Carter, you, as a religious man, served as president of the United States. Were there ever times when your faith and your role were in conflict?" And his answer—I think I commented on this earlier—was very thoughtful. Finally he said, "Yes. There were times." He went on to explain.

For me, there were times when there was a conflict. There was a time when some faculty members saw it as a conflict. I remember a motion to censure the president on the floor of the Faculty Senate for the practice of returning thanks before meals and with guests in the president's home because, after all, the house was a public space. I thought it was a silly discussion and treated it as such. But I think the intent was not silly, and I honor that intent.

I was asked, from time to time, to serve in various roles in the church, which I thought would put me in conflict. For example, I was asked to serve as a trustee of the seminary from which I graduated. I told the president that once I had retired from office I'd be pleased to serve, and I did, but not while in office. Probably, the one point at which I stretched it was for very close friends, faculty members and their families. I did from time to time exercise my prerogative as an ordained minister to perform weddings. Although I didn't keep it a secret, the services were rarely noted, except by the people involved.

Suddenly in the closing years of my presidency, someone who thought he had an axe to grind and a cause went into a public tirade and crusade that all the people for whom I had performed a wedding service were clearly not married because I was not legally authorized to perform marriages. He was wrong. I had gone to Judge [Gordon B.] Gray, early on, when I was asked to marry someone. I have in my file the legal document, the authority being a judge, that I was authorized as an ordained minister to marry couples. This yahoo who launched the campaign had another agenda; he was squelched when I produced the document. I think that there were times when I felt a tension between the desires to reach out to someone in mercy, because every student who is dismissed in a judicial case ultimately has the right of appeal to the president. But as Jimmy Carter said, "We are a nation of laws rather than men." I was obligated to abide by the rules.

DM: As I recall, it was quietly known that you were an ordained minister. Do you have any idea how many marriages you actually—

CP: I really did try to limit it to people with whom I was very close. There were some wonderful occasions. Well, that's another whole subject.

DM: But it's something, I'm sure, that brought you joy. It certainly brought others joy and a nice break from other duties. You had the opportunity and ability to take that break.

CP: Yes. One of the more memorable occasions, on a very hot day, I was laboring away in Cutler, and Alan Geiger, my very able assistant, came in and said, "Charlie, a graduate is out in the waiting room and wants to see you, and I think you really ought to talk to him." So I said, "Well send him in, then."

And he came in, and he said, "My name is _____, and I am a graduate of Ohio, and my wife is also a graduate. We were married two days ago by a civil authority, but my wife's family insists that until she has a church wedding she's not, indeed, married. So we decided to go through the service a second time. This time, with the benefit of clergy, I had arranged with a local minister to come to Galbreath Chapel to perform the ceremony. We had been waiting for two hours in the heat, and both families were getting a little bit antsy and a conflict is beginning to emerge. Please help us."

I said, "What do you want me to do?" He said, "I understand that you are a clergyman. We'd like very much for you to come and perform the ceremony." I said, "I don't have my book of common worship, but I think I can do it."

So I went over to Galbreath. I took the bride's family downstairs and calmed them down and got them quiet. Then I went upstairs and got the groom's family to quiet down. Then we had a wedding. They left with a glow, and both families were completely pleased, and I went back to my office and continued the day.

DM: [laughs] Speaking of Galbreath Chapel, I don't know how usual or unusual it is to have a chapel structure on a public university campus. I do know something about the background of that chapel that was provided by John Galbreath in memory of his wife. This was during John Baker's presidency, and John was very careful to thank John Galbreath for the funds for that chapel, but it would be nondenominational. I have witnessed a number of events in there, and I'm sure that you've seen a lot more there, but it's my impression that it has been carefully kept nondenominational.

CP: Yes, very definitely. I think it has been a quiet place on campus where students turn. John Galbreath was a long-time trustee and built the chapel in honor of his first wife, after she died. It's a miniature replica of a lovely church in London. It's an architecturally handsome building, oddly placed between two much larger buildings. And, I think, it is one of the highlights of the campus.

It's important. Having a chapel on campus is not that unusual, but Mr. Jefferson made the first statement with his insistence on a wall of separation. His architectural design for the University of Virginia was in blueprint and in structure a very strong statement. At the center of the green was the rotunda; it was the library, not a chapel. I think you can study his philosophy of higher education from the architectural design of the old campus with its academic discipline houses at the University of Virginia.

DM: I think you find similar things here. In our early years of Ohio University's existence, "chapel," as it was called, was required of all the students. Obviously it had a Presbyterian bent to it in those first years. I find it also interesting that Galbreath Chapel is, in essence, the site of the very first building of Ohio University, which was torn down after the erection of Cutler Hall.

CP: It actually burned down, I think.

DM: Really.

CP: Yes.

DM: OK. But it was a wood structure, so it was only temporary to begin with. But in those early years, everything happened within that building or Cutler Hall. This is one of the things that I find interesting about those early years of Ohio University and that Cutler Hall, or the Center Building as it was called at the time, had rooms for students to stay in. There were instruction rooms. It was the library. It was the scientific apparatus place and chapel was held there. Everything was done right there.

Another thing that I think I find really interesting about Ohio University, and, I think, explains a lot about Ohio University's charm and attraction, is that the University has maintained over two centuries now a center, and that center is the College Green.

CP: Yes. Well, you can walk the campus with a sense of history, if you are sensitive to that history. You not only see Manasseh Cutler, Reverend Lindley and others—Wilson was always my favorite—all these were university presidents, but you see Thomas Jefferson and Benjamin Franklin, and you have a sense that this University was part of that revolutionary history. It was built clearly with a mission. The colonial college and the postrevolutionary college had as its basic mission to educate literate and moral men. Religion was regarded as essential to that moral education for democracy.

DM: And we find, too, with the creation of Ohio University that ideal is set right there, at the very beginning.

CP: Well, there, you've used the word "ideal" again. [laughs]

DM: On purpose. [laughs] It's a continuation of the city on the hill. It's bringing it out to a new frontier, right after postrevolutionary America with this Northwest Territory, and Cutler and others in the Ohio Company felt very strongly that there had to be not only public schooling, but also a university, and that had to be established as early as possible.

CP: Yes, because as you know, there were seven colleges established before the revolution, and education was part of what the colonists set out to do, to make a New England.

DM: Right. Yes. I think in those days, there was a lot less separation between this idea of philosophy and religion, and they were really seen as very similar.

CP: We as a nation, or at least the leadership of the nation, had more in common with each other. Now we're far more diverse and rich, as a product of that diversity. I think the tradition that you see in the Campus Green and the sense of history is an important legacy that sets Ohio University apart.

DM: Well, I know you've traveled to many more university settings than I have, but I have rarely found, west of the Appalachians, a more beautiful campus, a more accommodating, a more feel good place. Without knowing a whole lot about it, as soon as I saw Ohio University that is what struck me.

CP: I can tell endless stories of many students who testified to that fact. I remember one graduation day, after we finished all the ceremonies, this was early in my presidency, and we had recently torn down Howard Hall, and I think Super Hall was down. Our busy day was finished, and my wife and I were back at 29 Park Place in sort of an, "Ah!" We were getting comfortable, and there was a knock on the door. A student was standing there with her robe still on. As soon as I opened the door she said, "There is just one thing I want to say to you. You are not going to tear down any more buildings on my campus."

DM: [laughs]

CP: [laughs] And I think some students feel that way.

DM: Had Ewing Hall been torn down yet?

CP: Oh, yes. It was gone.

DM: Well, interestingly enough at least two of those buildings were pretty incongruous to the campus anyway.

CP: Yes.

DM: We've talked about these things. So many campuses have taken the attitude that they need to modernize and you end up with mixed architectural styles and so forth—

CP: There are various philosophies of campus architecture. The contrasting philosophy, I think, is a completely defensible one. It says that every time you build you should build to reflect the era in which the building was built. So you get campuses, even some of the great old campuses, with buildings that reflect different eras.

DM: I've seen that and looked at a few when I was preparing to go to college, and personally I found them and felt them to be cold. It's a visual thing, but it's also a feeling, and that was not the case at all when I came to Ohio University.

CP: Yes. That captured me right from my first visit, too.

DM: I think it is—and this goes back to at least John Baker if not before —a conscious decision to be sure that this campus and its buildings, and even with the newer buildings, reflect in some way the older buildings.

President Ping seated on the College Green wall with the historic Cutler Hall in the background, 1979.

CP: Doug, I may have told the story, but I'll tell it again because it reflects how important it is to me. I was being pressed by one of the Big Ten universities. They were searching for a president. Finally the chairman of the board called me in the morning and said, "Charlie, we are ready to meet and to elect you president, but before we take that vote, we want to be sure that you will accept it." I replied, "I will give you an answer by noon." I had spent a couple of days on that campus, and the discussion had gone on for weeks. So I said, "I will call you back, I promise, before noon."

I decided to take a walk. I went uptown. As I came back and was walking up the hill toward Cutler, I stopped and stood there thinking. I had just come back from the other campus and its administration building—it's a lovely campus, and they have preserved much of the environment, but the administration building is a huge glass and steel structure. The president's office is very spacious. It has all sorts of wonderful accommodations, but I remember standing there thinking, "You know a president could be there, then leave, and they could change the partitions around, so no one would ever know he'd been there." I sort of chuckled to myself and stood there for another minute. I said to myself, "I really like going to my office in Cutler. I relish those walks in front of Alden and that small garden behind Cutler and Alden. I relish the buildings and my office." So, I went back to my office, and I called, and said, "No."

DM: There's an intimacy here, isn't there?

CP: Yes.

DM: We've talked some about philosophy and some about religion and we've touched on Ohio University being a public university. We're, of course, well aware there are private universities in the country as well. I think this country may very well have the highest number of universities of any other country in the world, for all I know. And they run the gamut—from very small to quite large. The largest, apparently, is just up the road here. They all have different ideas and directions about what they're doing. So, what is the university's place in society, or in American society, to start with? And if you want to, let's look at a global perspective?

CP: That's a large order question—

DM: I know. [laughs]

CP: I have made many speeches and written many articles on the subject. Let me speak to the question you're asking. We were the first land grant college; long before the Morrill Land Grant Act, we were the model. We belong to that tradition, which has as a public mission to prepare people for the needs of society.

If you read the Land Grant Act carefully, it says, "to liberally educate." So, it combines both the historic mission of humanizing through education and preparing people to be able to serve the needs of society. The growth of public universities in the nineteenth century brought them gradually to a dominant position in the twentieth century. In terms of enrollment—80 percent of the students are in public higher education. We have grown to a size that we can provide a broad access for the children of "the industrial classes." That's a quote from the Land Grant Act of the 1860s.

The Land Grant Act affirmed the first mission of the public university was to educate the children of the industrial class. They were to open the door of opportunity for the children of those who came to this country as immigrants, and who had very little or no education. Their children could go on to become the teachers, the doctors, the lawyers, the judges, and the legislators. There was nothing that they couldn't do. This is the sense of a very central role.

Then with the difficult years leading up to the Second World War, the universities took on a larger public mission. Franklin Roosevelt made the decision that since we were gearing up for a war that was going to be technologically sophisticated this country would use the research capabilities that were already in existence on university campuses.

So a huge federal investment opened up the role of research in the public university as well as in the private university. Johns Hopkins, the Ivy Leagues, and public universities like Michigan and Berkeley were the largest recipients. They are still being funded to do research in the public interest. Now, basic research is in the national interest, for example, in the development of the atomic bomb. War is a painful stimulus; the nation's interests have moved on to issues of public health and a broad array of social public problems.

DM: Well, and then the next step is the GI Bill and the real, serious broadening—

CP: Yes. I came into college with all these returning veterans. It was a different era. I was on a football team where, I think, I was the youngest starting player in my freshman year and my senior year. I don't know that that's true, but the end starting next to me was thirty-six or thirty-seven years old, a veteran being supported by the GI bill.

Some of my close friends, college and seminary classmates, were returning servicemen. One of them was a major who started college late in life. It had never occurred to him before that going to college was either possible or desirable. I think the GI bill was instrumental in changing that.

And under Lyndon Johnson's leadership, and the passing of a Higher Education Act, the federal government opened higher education more broadly by providing funding to remove economic barriers.

DM: We have several things going on here that could easily be major conflicts. The tradition, out of Europe, was the university was to train elites, those who move into the highest levels of society. That has certainly been used here in the United States, but then this other idea of a public university and what that all means suggests the possible conflict between general undergraduate education versus graduate education and research.

CP: I think the role of the university is to prepare the leadership for society, and to educate the brightest and best students for their role—the role of leadership. The base is so broad that every institution in society is affected. We are a democracy, and there's no reason to assume that the child of a mechanic will grow up to be a mechanic, as is true in many of the more traditional societies. The child of a mechanic may very well become a judge. Colleges of opportunity help them achieve that end.

DM: All the students have to do is take advantage of that, right?

CP: Sure. You know some find their way, but it's relatively a small percentage—to leadership roles without that education. This country has tried to ensure that we would have universal access to higher education— not universal postsecondary education, but a broad access with geographic and economic barriers removed.

DM: The United States has done a great deal of working in that direction with all the grants, loan programs, and special interest rates, and so forth—

CP: And the number of institutions. We have over 3,500 colleges and universities in this country. A student can find one that serves his or her needs, and one that will admit the student.

DM: I think it is a wonderful thing. It's, I think, one of the major factors in what makes the Unites States the United States.

CP: Yes. It is the democratic tradition in higher education.

DM: And, too, I think it's been wonderful to see lots of interaction amongst colleges and universities, or postsecondary institutions amongst themselves within the United States but also on a global scale. Other countries have many fewer institutions of higher education or postsecondary education in the first place, but the United States is the choice, in many cases, for people from other parts—

CP: Yes.

DM: of the world.

CP: Large international populations on campus were a post–World War II development. We've always had some exchanges. We had Japanese students here at Ohio in the nineteenth century, together with Chinese students and others. It's an important part of the Ohio University tradition. But more broadly, it was the post–World War II years, with much of the developed world completely devastated that led to the opening of doors in the US.

Senator Fulbright and the act that bears his name opened doors in both directions and a flow began. It wasn't a large flow, initially. One of my roles in graduate school—I was the house master of the Men's Graduate Center at Duke. There were few women in the graduate and professional schools back then; now they dominate enrollment in medicine and law and many other areas. One of the things beginning to appear in the early '50s was international students sponsored by various groups. And Fulbright students started coming this way.

My role at Duke was to ensure that the international graduate students housed on campus were reasonably adjusted. One person, part-time, on a major university campus—there really were not very many international students. I became close friends with some of the international students. Many graduate students had a tortured experience once here. They were absolutely fluent in their native languages, of course, already well-established scholars. Suddenly they had to read a whole shelf of books in English for a graduate seminar. It became overwhelming. The numbers have grown and grown in the decades that followed, until now, there's about a half million international students studying in America. Most now arrive completely fluent in English, although some require special training in English as a second language. While a modest percentage of American students study abroad. Ohio is working to increase the numbers from Ohio University taking advantage of that opportunity.

DM: When I first came to Ohio University in the fall of 1969, I noticed two minorities: international students and also African American students.

I found it also interesting that the numbers were about the same. Less than 10 percent of Ohio University's undergraduate numbers were African Americans and about 10 percent of the overall student population was international. Universities and our society made a major correction in the effort to enroll minorities in most recent times. Because African Americans weren't terribly welcome at universities for a long, long time.

CP: Part of our history is the proud moment when John Newton Templeton, in 1828, graduated. He was probably the third or fourth African American to take a degree from an American college. But our history is mixed, if you really read the record carefully. As you move through the post–Civil War period, and into the first half of the twentieth century, frankly, the American conscience was not stirred.

The events of the 1960s, the civil rights movement, and the struggles in Mississippi and throughout the South quickened the conscience of all campuses. One student, enrolling at Ole Miss, required some five thousand federal troops and several hundred federal marshals, and two days of rioting. The student population of Ole Miss is probably 20 percent or so minorities today. The football team is probably a higher percentage. There were no African Americans on the football team in the early '60s. And, it was a struggle everywhere.

Subtle and terribly damaging forms of discrimination continue, but the mind-set has changed. Not completely, but I think campuses not only welcome, but work at enrolling minorities—this one certainly does—recruiting African American students, and increasingly, I think, students of Mexican and Latin American origin. And one of the great things about Ohio University is—you mentioned—this presence of international students. This population continues to be an important fact, even as the linkage to campuses around the world grows. That's the world we live in, and we need to prepare students for this new global reality.

DM: And many opportunities for students to branch out, if only they seek it. Another minority, or considered a minority for many, many years, would be women. It took Ohio University seventy or so years to even admit that women existed.

CP: Yes.

DM: [laughs] Back then, Margaret Boyd had to register as M. Boyd to hide her gender, and it took even longer for the first African American woman to graduate. But Ohio University, not unlike many other universities in the United States, has gone far not only to admit women, but also to broaden their opportunities in terms of what they study.

CP: Yes, it has. It's now true that women are a majority on college campuses and in most of the graduate schools and disciplines. Like the African American, change was a matter of quickening the conscience. We can take pride in Margaret Boyd. We were early, and there weren't many campuses that were prepared to admit women in the 1860s.

In fact, one of the great presidents of Harvard, in his 1869 inaugural address, Charles Eliot, said Harvard would not admit women, and he explained why. There was no evidence that women were intellectually capable. He said, "They may very well be, but we need the evidence." I think it's a marvelous description of how far we have come, and that by 2010 the president of Harvard University was a woman. And I'm sure Charles Eliot would be very pleased, because she's a very able and competent scholar as well.

DM: And she's been able to prove it. [laughs]

CP: Yes. And I think this is what has changed most. With the emergence of public education, this nation, if it was going to offer universal primary education and universal secondary education, had to have a host of teachers. Teaching was one of the keys to women's access to college. Great numbers of women came to the campuses in the last quarter of the nineteenth century to serve this expanding public education.

DM: We saw that on this campus as well—

CP: Yes.

DM: with the summer sessions and the huge increase in the College of Education—which consisted almost entirely of women. Then around the same post–World War II period, I remember seeing comments at Ohio University and other places of a concern amongst many administrators and administrations—a fear that they were becoming women's colleges with so few men on campus, and whether men would come back. Well, of course, they came back. But then women, for a short time, were put back into secretarial and—

CP: Yes.

DM: teacher-type roles and then—

CP: It was the opportunities to enter professions that really opened university doors fully, including a stronger presence on college faculty. I see that as a very important development. There were a lot of women on campus in the 1920s when women gained the right to vote. But really, the only two professions that welcomed women at the time were teaching and nursing.

Here I was, as the house master of the men's graduate center at Duke, in the second half of the 1950s, and there were no women in divinity school, of all places; there were no women in the law school; there were no women in med school, and so on. The only facility housing single students on the campus was the Men's Graduate Center. There was no provision for women graduates or professional school students other than nursing. My, how the world has changed.

Johns Hopkins, two years ago, reported that the majority entering the medical school were women. At our medical school, the majority for the last several years has been women.

DM: Then people like Jeanette Grasselli Brown look to encourage women in professions such as the sciences and engineering.

CP: Yes. She was a graduate of Ohio, a wonderful trustee, and a great friend. Jenny Grasselli Brown held the highest office by a woman in the

SOHIO organization. She was the director of their research labs. She's a physical chemist, internationally renowned, recognized and honored by governments and universities, and a wonderful person.

DM: I had mentioned earlier your own efforts to help break through the glass ceiling for women and other minorities too with your own administration. I think this a very important thing for this University, as well as on a broader scale. Because that was one of the final impediments for women, which was not to be able to be right at the very top.

CP: And now a sizable number of the Ivy League schools have female presidents.

DM: My, how things change. [laughs]

CP: Yes.

DM: And for the better. Let's move to your postpresidential time. Perhaps we could start by getting into the circumstances that led up to your retirement in 1994, and then move along from there.

CP: Retirement . . . We had finished our second very successful national campaign—The Third Century Campaign. Our goal was to raise $100 million, and thanks to the good leadership of Jack Ellis and the efforts of a host of volunteers, we raised $130-some million. More importantly, we gathered a whole core of new alumni supporters.

I think the campus had regained the respect of high school counselors, parents, and certainly students. The numbers of applications supports that. We had had a lot of good press. We had regained our rightful place. We were recognized as a research university and a member of the Association of Research Libraries, our College of Osteopathic Medicine was prospering, and on and on.

I had had chronic orthopedic problems for many years. They had whittled on my knees beginning in my high school years and all through college. They were a source of great pain, off and on. And as we moved through the late '80s, the pain became increasingly difficult to live with. Doctors at the Cleveland Clinic had been telling me for ten years that the only way I was going to get relief was to replace both knees. Then they told me, "But for us to work on the knees, you have to have two functioning shoulders." So we agreed that they would start with the shoulders. They repaired one shoulder; and six months later, they repaired my other shoulder. During that time, I got clearance to chair a commission in Africa, on the condition that my wife would go with me to insure that I would not pick up anything heavier than a pencil or a pen. It was a very painful rehab. But I was able to function.

After a year of shoulders, the time had come—I was having heavy internal bleeding in my knees, and they would swell to the point that it was excruciatingly painful. I remember dear Dr. Sprague, our family physician, coming to the house one night—in response to Claire's plea—and going up to the third floor where I was sitting in my favorite chair watching television. Trying to give me some relief, he gave me a very strong injection. Suddenly, I couldn't stand up, and there was no bed on the third floor. So he got on the phone with the football coach, and he had a couple of big athletes come up, and they carried me down to the bedroom.

Anyway, I went to the Cleveland Clinic, and I had both knees done at the same time—total replacement. Then blood clots and other complications followed the surgery. I spent two and a half weeks in the Cleveland Clinic. I came back and went through six months of very difficult rehab. Thanks to the loving support of my wife, who was infinitely patient, and the steady work of Skip Vosler and others, I regained the use of my legs.

Skip and others would come to the house and work with me because I wasn't able to go down the stairs. We would strain and sweat to get a degree more flexion, or a degree more extension. The physical plant put in a chair seat, so I could get up and down the back stairs. On crutches, I tried to go back to Cutler and pick up my work. And eventually, I did. But I had six months of walking the campus with crutches. This is not a very safe campus for crutches.

DM: No.

CP: The brick sidewalks have all sorts of peril. Anyway, I was beginning to recuperate from the knee replacements, when I was at an alumni event in the Konneker Alumni Center. I realized that suddenly my one leg was numb. I had been standing and greeting people for about an hour. When the time came to go home, I had to drag that leg and I thought, "Well these blankity-blank knees. Something's gone wrong."

I immediately had a new round of X-rays and scans. Finally, the physicians at the Cleveland Clinic said, "Your knees are working fine, but you have two herniated disks in your back, and you have a narrowing of the spinal column." Further they said, "The only way the problems are to be corrected is to do some major back surgery." Needless to say, I was a little discouraged and decided that I had neither the energy nor the patience to continue as president.

Ralph Schey, who was then chairman of the board, came up to our summer place and spent the day with me talking. He said, "Charlie, what we need to do is hire people to do all the parts of the job that you really don't like to do, and then you could stay in office." To which I replied, "Ralph, the parts of the job I'd have you hiring people for is the legislature, at the start, and some other things like fund-raising, all of which require a president." He said, "That's what I do with my company. I bring people on board as key staff." And I said, "Well, I'm surrounded by good people, but still it takes a president to speak for the institution. And so I think it's time to replace me."

I had hoped to stay twenty years, but that proved impossible. The trustees graciously supported me as I applied for and received a grant to go back to Southern Africa. I told the trustees I would stay in office and try to conduct the office well until my successor was on board, and then I would turn over the keys to the place and go happily on my way.

The board, in essence, said, "We'd like you to go happily on your way for a year and then come back. You have some unfinished business here." I was pleased and flattered. The "unfinished business," of course, was two endowed programs—the Cutler Scholars and the Institute for the Teaching of the Humanities. I insisted that I wanted to once again be a philosophy professor and teach full-time. The trustees agreed and said they would support me in the effort to teach and take on the two tasks, and they did with staff and funding.

Both the Cutler Scholars and the Ping Institute needed leadership to get off the ground. I had been working, with Will Konneker's encouragement and support, to identify a model program to train gifted and dedicated students for the tasks of leadership. The program design and governance was formally approved by the foundation board about the time I retired and was waiting for me when I returned. Endowment was in place and earnings beginning to flow in support of Cutler activity. The Ping Institute was dedicated to the teaching of the humanities, but time was needed to build up enough funds to allow the appointment of the faculty and fellows who would develop the program.

I, literally, turned over the keys to university buildings to Bob Glidden in a ceremony, July 1994, on the walk in front of Cutler. Now we were determined to leave and to get completely out of the way of the new president. First, we went to our cottage in Northern Michigan, and from there, we left for Africa to take up my appointment as a Fulbright Senior Research Scholar for Southern Africa. We spent most of our time in Namibia and Botswana. I was attempting to explore in interviews and conversations expectations for their universities and to determine conflicts or tensions, if any, in several sets of expectations. In both countries, I was able to interview the president and other leading government officials; church, labor, and business leaders; as well as faculty, administrators, and students. It was an interesting project and revealed some troubling tensions. All of which I addressed in a couple of articles when I returned. One of the highlights of the year was when the Konnekers came to Africa and, as we had done often in the past, the four of us took a holiday. We spent a few delightful days in a game park in Namibia; drove down the sharp ravines of the Kalahari Desert to Walvis Bay and Swakopmund; toured the Cape Town area; took an excursion Blue Train trip to Bulawayo, Cecil Rhodes's summer home, burial site, and now museum; went to Victoria Falls; and then on to Gaborone, Botswana.

Claire and I returned to Athens, settled in a home on a country lane, and for the next few years I taught full time in the philosophy department. Teaching has a strong pull on my heart, and I'm pleased that at the end of my career I could return to the classroom as a professor. My colleagues in the department even honored me, I think, by electing me to membership on the Tenure and Promotion Committee.

In addition to teaching full time, I was expected to lead the way in getting two endowed programs off the ground—The Cutler Scholars Program and The Ping Institute for the Teaching of the Humanities. The assignments were a joy to undertake, and I note with great pride that both the Cutler Scholars and the institute are alive and prospering.

My life in retirement was full of many things. As I had promised the president of the Louisville Seminary, once retired, I went on the board of trustees. I took an active role on the Louisville board, and a few years after joining the board, sadly, found myself embroiled in a termination for cause of the sitting president and the search for his successor. Following my Fulbright experience, I was asked to serve on the Fulbright Scholars Board and for years chaired the Committee for Southern Africa. This entailed regular meetings and, annually, the careful review of a great mountain of proposals from applicants who wanted to be Fulbright Scholars in Southern Africa. It was both an honor and a pleasure to serve. I also was on several other boards, including the Muskingum College Trustees.

Just as I was about to retire, I was approached by several friends who were national leaders of higher education. The chancellor of the SUNY system said to me, "An important organization needs new leadership for its board of directors. The organization has some problems, and we think you are just the right person to be the chair, given your long-standing commitment to internationalizing campuses." "This would be," they said in concert and individually, "an ideal assignment for you in retirement." So I looked at the people involved, Senator Fulbright was the honorary chair of the board right up to his death, and I looked at the organization's history, and I agreed to go on the board of the Council on International Educational Exchange as chair of the board.

Well, it turned out to be a richly rewarding, although time-consuming, experience, and it continued for twelve years. CIEE was a troubled organization; I was somewhat familiar with troubled organizations. To start, council had a long-serving president who had been with the organization in various roles right from the start of the Fulbright Exchange program. He loved council and served it faithfully as president, but he managed CIEE with a benign neglect, spending half his year in Paris and half in New York. By the time I joined the board, CIEE was a major provider of study abroad programs around the globe as well as inbound work and study opportunities for thousands of international students. CIEE, in addition, operated Council Travel, a $200 million-a-year business selling tickets to students and faculty.

I spent six months working closely with the president trying to understand the financial reports submitted to the board. They were complex, confused, and confusing. I studied them carefully and began to sense that CIEE was really bankrupt, but the board didn't believe it because of the huge cash float generated by the travel company. The float was money owed at some future date, but that didn't seem to matter.

Before we could replace the president, the governance structure of CIEE needed to be overhauled. The board functioned not like a board but more like a faculty senate. The board spent endless time discussing issues but found it difficult to make timely or unpopular decisions. The board included thirty-eight dedicated people, most of them campus directors of study abroad from the best universities in the country and most of them infected with serious faculty mind-sets. They had been talking about various schemes for the reorganization of governance for years without concluding how to accomplish that task.

We convened a special meeting dedicated to governance in Santa Fe and spent two days discussing a proposal, which had won favor, to create an academic advisory board and a smaller corporate board of directors. There were scenes of people weeping at one moment and then arguing with great anger the next. I had begun to despair of ever getting a decision, so I said, "We have talked and talked to the point of near exhaustion.

255

I think it's time to vote." So I called for a few moments of silence and reflection and then a vote. To my utter amazement, when the paper ballots were counted, it was a unanimous "Yes!" The board had voted itself out of existence and established a corporate structure to provide fiscal direction and oversight and policy planning for CIEE. For an academic, it was an incredible moment!

A new board of directors was organized and launched a search for a president. To our great good fortune, we were able to recruit a talented man, at home both on the campus and in the world of finance, a Harvard DBA with just the right experience. Stevan Trooboff quickly began to make a difference. CIEE was soon operating on a sound financial basis, and there was a new, bright, able, and aggressive core of people supporting the president.

Steve and I worked together for over a decade in what was one of the most satisfying relations of my retirement. In the next few years, with Steve leading the way, the board approved: the timely sale of Council Travel to the Irish student travel organization; an effort to draw the whole worldwide organization into a shared sense of mission; a decision to close offices in Paris, Berlin, Madrid, and London; the moving of the corporate offices from expensive space in midtown Manhattan to Portland, Maine; the building of a structure in Portland to house all CIEE corporate offices; transparent financial reporting that allowed the board to exercise its fiduciary responsibilities; and gradually, the building of a healthy reserve. The list could be expanded, but the decade was obviously a heady volunteer activity for a retired president serving as chair.

I decided I ought to get out of the way, so I retired from the CIEE board. To my surprise and delight at my last annual conference—the conference is a large gathering of study abroad people from around the globe—the board announced the creation of a foundation in my name with income from its two-million-dollar endowment to fund research into study abroad, public advocacy, and scholarships. Ro Fallon, the new chair of the CIEE board, is a retired bank executive, an Ohio University graduate, and a very effective advocate for internationalizing universities.

This has been a long narrative, but you asked, Doug, that I talk about what I have been doing in retirement besides having more time to enjoy my family and time to spend at our cottage on Grand Traverse Bay in Northern Michigan. The truth is, I enjoy talking about Fulbright programs and CIEE and, when asked, I go on and on and on . . .

Now, let's return to the Ohio University campus. After retiring as president, I taught full time in the philosophy department for several years, and then decided I had to teach on a more limited schedule and began to teach part time in philosophy and in the Higher Education PhD Program in the College of Education. I continue to teach but limit myself now to one graduate seminar each year. I remain active with the Cutler Scholars Program and the Institute for the Teaching of the Humanities. Both are ably led as I said earlier, Cutler by Butch Hill and the institute by Tom Carpenter. I also serve on a few campus committees, for example, the Baker Peace Studies Committee. I think I have now managed to resign or retire from all outside boards and committees.

This has been an inordinately long answer to your question, but to answer, I had to talk about eighteen years of my life. I hope it supports my assertion that I have had an active, satisfying retirement.

DM: [laughs] I was going to say, "Is this really retirement?"

CP: My wife insists that I failed retirement.

DM: [laughs] Maybe that's the only thing you've ever failed at in your career.

CP: That's not true, but thank you.

DM: [laughs] What happens from here? This is the late spring and almost early summer of 2011, and tomorrow you are leaving for a four-month hiatus at your wonderful breakaway place in Michigan, and then you're back, and then what?

Charles Ping, looking every bit the former athlete, in a rare leisure moment vacationing at the Ping cottage on Grand Traverse Bay, Michigan, 1975.

CP: Well, I hope, as long as I'm able and feel I can contribute, to work with the Cutler Scholars. When I'm on campus, I meet with the weekly Cutler colloquia. I continue to be active with the Ping Institute or at least have the privilege of meeting with the changing generations of faculty and fellows of the Ping Institute and following their activities. And I teach. I try to make it to my office with a fair degree of regularity. Occasionally, I'm a presence at various events on campus. I presented an award at the Student Leadership Awards banquet last year. I occasionally speak at dinners. Recently I was inducted to the ROTC Hall of Fame; that's a story that goes back to my early years here. And, in all of this, I think, I have stayed out of the president's way.

We are good friends with President McDavis and Deborah. I try to be supportive and helpful in any way I can. Sadly, my duties frequently entail honoring the service and the life of people at their death; I per-

(*From left*) Ohio University Foundation Board trustee and CIEE chair, Ro Fallon; President Charles Ping; and Foundation Board trustee chair, Laura Brege, at the dinner honoring Vern Alden on February 4, 2011, at Alden Library.

form occasional weddings. Just to walk the campus is to be a part of a remarkable University. This is a great passion.

DM: I'm sure it has been a great satisfaction as well. Thank you very much, and enjoy your summer.

CP: Thank you.

INDEX

Page references in italics indicate photographs on those pages.